YALE STUDIES IN ENGLISH

BENJAMIN CHRISTIE NANGLE, EDITOR

VOLUME 156

WYCHERLEY'S DRAMA

A Link in the Development of English Satire

by Rose A. Zimbardo

New Haven and London, Yale University Press, 1965

Copyright © 1965 by Yale University.
Designed by John O. C. McCrillis,
set in Garamond type,
and printed in the United States of America by
The Carl Purington Rollins Printing-Office of
the Yale University Press, New Haven, Connecticut.
All rights reserved. This book may not be
reproduced, in whole or in part, in any form
(except by reviewers for the public press),
without written permission from the publishers.

Library of Congress catalog card number: 65–11191

Published with assistance from the foundation
established in memory of William McKean Brown.

For the Great Zimbardos, Philip and Adam

Acknowledgments

THE CONCATENATION of events and influences in the life
of a book, as of a man, makes the full and proper acknowl-
edgment of debt impossible. Were I to be just, I should have
to begin by thanking those paragons, my parents, who, by
loving me despite my eccentricity, have allowed me to
cultivate the crooked eye that alone delights in satire.

My heaviest debts for intellectual goods received are to
Vera Lachmann and Asher Baizer. He, having lifted me
from mushroomhood, shaped my thought and first taught
me to appreciate Augustan formalism. I am particularly
indebted to his doctoral dissertation, "The Theory of Imitation in English Neoclassical Criticism" (New York University, 1960), for my discussion of imitation.

The foundation of this book was originally presented to
Yale University as a doctoral dissertation.

I cannot gauge the extent of my debt to Yale. When I
was still one of the "culturally disadvantaged," I looked to
it as to the Heavenly City. It racked me, but it has never
disappointed me. Three men particularly embody Yale for
me. To Talbot Donaldson I am grateful because he is not
only a gentleman and a scholar but a gambler as well.
William K. Wimsatt taught me to despise shoddy thought,
especially my own. His voice has come to be my internal
critic, and it is for his good opinion that I always secretly
strive. To Eugene M. Waith I am most grateful, for he
presents the ideal in scholarship, in teaching, in intellectual
grace toward which all my imitations aspire. Whatever in
this book has value was inspired and nurtured by him. What

is gross or imperfect is my own and marks the extent to which I fall short of my model.

I am grateful to Benjamin Nangle for helping to prepare the manuscript for press.

My debts at City College are also great. I thank the Scholarship Committee for the grant-in-aid that helped me to revise and expand my original conception. Edgar Johnson, my chairman and friend, has always come to my rescue in true knightly fashion with a book, a grant application, or a legal loophole. To my students, who provide a testing ground for my ideas, I am also grateful. They never allow me to slip into attitudes.

I thank my friend Ira Grushow for reading the manuscript in its ugly duckling adolescence and for laughing me to scorn when my ideas grow to folly.

As for the Great Zimbardo, I thank him for being the Great Zimbardo. It is with some surprise that I find he has coaxed and bullied, petted and pinched me into a book. No less a hero than he could have borne me through this or could, indeed, have listened so often to the opening paragraph.

R. A. Z.

New York
June, 1964

Contents

As pointed and severe as he is in his writings, in his Temper he has all the softness of the tenderest disposition; gentle and inoffensive to every man in his particular character; he only attacks Vice as a public Enemy, compassionating the wound he is under necessity to probe.

—George Granville, Baron Lansdowne

1. Abolishing the Cliché

CRITICISM of Restoration comedy is unique in that since 1698[1] it has centered upon an extraliterary question. The history of this criticism records one long contention between those critics who dismiss the plays as immoral[2] and those who seek to clear them of that charge. This diversion of attention from literary to moral issues has had very unfortunate consequences. Detractors, in the heavy armor of moral prejudice, have damned the plays without granting them that objective consideration accorded other areas of literature that allows a work of art to reveal its moral position in terms of its own aesthetic design. Admirers have been no less blind. In trying to prove the comedies harmless, they have rendered them trivial. Constructing their theories upon sociological grounds, they have succeeded in convincing us that the plays are either pointless—"a holiday from the sublime and beautiful, the coarse and real"[3]—or mindless—products of a "photographic realism"[4] that reflect without commentary the conjured carnival of rakes and wenches that is supposed to be Restoration life.

Beyond the error of undervaluing the plays, of which any critical approach to any period might be guilty, there is a

---

1. The year of Jeremy Collier's *A Short View of the Profaneness and Immorality of the English Stage.*
2. This charge has been made as recently as 1956. Cf. John Wain, "Restoration Comedy and its Modern Critics," *Essays in Criticism,* 6 (1956), 367–87.
3. John Palmer, *Comedy* (New York, 1914), p. 33.
4. Thomas Fujimura, *The Restoration Comedy of Wit* (Princeton, 1952), pp. 52, 53.

fundamental error far more grave. All blanket theories of
"Restoration comedy" rest upon the mistaken notion that
the Restoration period is a *cul de sac* in English cultural
history. This assumption has led critics to view the drama
of the period as homogeneous and unique, with the result
that they have not only yoked together writers of such
markedly different sensibility as Wycherley, Etherege, and
Congreve but have compounded their error by ignoring the
traditions antedating and stretching beyond the period in
which the plays were composed. When we have once
removed our blinders and allowed to each play the unpreju-
diced judgment to which it is entitled, we find that the
Restoration period is in the mainstream of English literary
history. Wycherley is revealed a writer of formal satire, who,
making use of both the Ancient English and Roman satiric
traditions, emends the Elizabethan conception of satiric
decorum and hands on to the age that follows his a conception of satire that was to be the foundation for the best
English achievement in that genre.

In contrast to the stark black and white of Wycherley's
satiric vision is the vision of Etherege, who, working in the
tradition of Pyrrhonistic skepticism,[5] investigates and tests
a reality which seventeenth-century science had called into
doubt. Congreve, taking yet another direction, writes in a
romantic tradition that is to ripen and finally rot into eighteenth-century sentimentalism.

The differences between the three major comic writers of
the period, as they define three separate traditions, can be
of more use to one who would understand their drama than
any false similarity or accident of chronology that has been
used to force them together. The term "Restoration comedy"
cannot be extended beyond its chronological sense. We are
being no more critical when we call the plays of Wycherley

5. Cf. Louis Bredvold, *The Intellectual Milieu of John Dryden* (Ann
   Arbor, 1934).

and Congreve Restoration comedies than we are when we call those of Jonson and Lyly Elizabethan comedies. Any generic usage of the term has been contrived to deal with a question outside the plays, and therefore outside the province of literary criticism.

Wycherley's plays have never been accommodated gracefully to a theory of Restoration comedy. He does not share even the surface resemblance of Etherege and Congreve. His design violates the typical love-chase pattern; his central characters do not arouse even the minimum sympathy required to raise them to the position of comic heroes; his style—lashing, abusive, and obscene by turns—is inconceivable in a play intended as a "holiday" from "the coarse and real." Yet, though these incongruities have led one critic to question the gentility of the playwright's birth[6] and another to admit that his plays "are exceptions in the Restoration comedy of manners canon,"[7] no one has been led to consider whether it is not the plays but rather our view of them that is distorted. Wycherley's mature plays cannot be fitted to the Procrustean bed of theory because not only are they not Restoration comedies, they are not comedies at all. Distorted when we try to make comedies of them, they are, ironically enough, quite regular, indeed formally perfect, when we recognize them as satires. The very qualities that render them unfit as comedy—decentralization of plot, absence of a hero, harshness of tone—are those that enable them to maintain perfectly the decorum of satire.

As I shall try in the succeeding chapters to show, *The Country Wife* and *The Plain Dealer* are attempts to realize in the dramatic mode a new English conception of formal satire. Though Wycherley's plays are pitifully few, they

6. Kathleen Lynch, *The Social Mode of Restoration Comedy* (New York, 1926), p. 174.
7. Dale Underwood, *Etherege and the 17th Century Comedy of Manners* (New Haven, 1957), p. 54 n.

show his persistent concern for and gradual mastery over form. Moreover, small as his contribution is in size, it is vitally important to the development of English satire. The study of Wycherley's form is best begun in the contrast between his central concern, general design, and method and those of Etherege and Congreve. The outline of his art begins to appear when we distinguish him from his contemporaries.

Etherege's central concern is to reproduce in drama the philosophical ambivalence that marks seventeenth-century thought. As Underwood shows, "The quest for reality . . . is the central concern [of his plays]. The concern is ideally vested in the comic hero because the circularity of his assumptions is without a center. Or to put the matter more accurately . . . his comic strengths lie in his negations but his negations cancel each other out."[8] To this I would add one qualification. "The quest for reality" implies the belief that there is an absolute reality. I would describe Etherege's purpose as the desire to weigh many perceptions of reality, the crux of thought lying in the belief that there are many realities of relative worth and that the state of man is one upon which many conflicting realities operate. The playwright's method is to pit different perceptions of reality against one another in an effort to recreate that complexity of vision that life affords. In *Timon,* the joint satire of Rochester and Buckingham, Etherege was twitted for his formlessness:

> Grammar and Rules of Art, he knows 'em not
> Yet writ two talking plays without one plot.

Nevertheless, it is the very abandonment of traditional comic design that enables him to capture the multiplicity and contradiction of the realities he describes. Consider his method in *The Man of Mode,* his most perfect play. The central action, the pursuit of the clever coquette Harriet by

8. Ibid., p. 49.

Dorimant the libertine, is by no means a "plot" in the usual sense; much of the play does not even contribute to this action. It is, rather, the central among many conflicts of perception. In the loosest of structures, scenes that are almost separable are arranged to balance or contrast to the end either of illuminating contradictory aspects of the hero's personality or of affording some new angle from which to consider the many realities in the play.

Briefly recounted, the tale is of Dorimant, a rake, who is in the process of discarding an old mistress, Mrs. Loveit, and acquiring two new ones, Bellinda and Harriet. He is able to seduce Bellinda, but Harriet proves his match in wit and he finds that he can win her only in marriage. To gain her end, the capture and taming of Dorimant, Harriet must outwit both Dorimant and her mother, who, as a guardian of virtue, is terrified by the very mention of Dorimant's name. Harriet's mother is anxious to marry her to Bellair, the sentimental lover of Emilia, but Harriet and Bellair are in league to prevent such a match. Bellair and Emilia, sentimentally in love, must overcome the efforts of Bellair's father to match his son's fortune with Harriet's and marry Emilia himself. As even so brief a survey as this shows, multiple conflicts of interest create a design exactly suited to Etherege's comic purpose. Scenes serve only to throw the characters, who are matched pairs of opposites, into contrast to reveal the conflict between the ideas, or perceptions for which they stand. Thus Mrs. Loveit, or rash intemperance, is juxtaposed with Harriet, or controlling judgment. The values of a former age, in love with ceremony, are embodied in Harriet's mother and are contrasted with the values of a younger generation which uses ceremony only for disguise, illustrated in Dorimant's posing as Mr. Courtage. Sentimental lovers are weighed against clever ones and then, ironically enough, both the clever and the sentimental fall victims to custom.

Much of what forms the real interest of the play does not contribute at all to the central action. For example, we are given, in three separate scenes, three vantages of Dorimant. In his first scene with Mrs. Loveit we see him in all of his petty malice. He deliberately drives a woman whose favors he has enjoyed to extremes of uncontrollable anger and then amuses himself with the spectacle of her passion. On the other hand, his scenes with Bellinda reveal the libertine spirit in its most beguiling form; here Dorimant is a devilish, charming rake. Finally, with Harriet, Dorimant comes near to being a genuinely sentimental lover. But we are not to think that these changes mark a progress toward virtue. No sooner do we glimpse the sentimental side of Dorimant than he reverts to rakishness. For example, having admitted to himself that the love he feels for Harriet is different from that aroused by his usual amorous encounters, he pulls himself up with the sharp reminder that he is a libertine still.

> The hour is almost come I appointed Bellinda
> I am not so foppishly in love here to forget.
> I am flesh and blood yet.   [IV, i, 4][9]

We are never permitted to settle into a single view of Dorimant. And to further complicate our perception, Etherege throws Sir Fopling Flutter, an imitation libertine, into the action to set off Dorimant's true libertinism. Yet the consequence of this contrast is further complication. As in life, the line of demarcation between true and false is blurred, and rather than defining true libertinism the contrast raises further questions about what it is. Characters not only contrast but blend, and our final impression is of multiple realities in constant flux.

Using the same method that he uses to complicate char-

9. All references to Etherege's plays are to *The Dramatic Works of Sir George Etherege,* ed. H. F. E. Brett-Smith (2 vols. Oxford, 1927).

acter, Etherege creates the impression of a multifold reality in his plot. Scenes that bear no direct relation to the action are casually introduced. The opening scene is an excellent example. Dorimant's toilette is interrupted by the appearance of the orangewoman and the shoemaker. A contrast is struck between that class of society that must work for a living and that whose sole employment is pleasure. Yet no sooner is the contrast made than it is ironically reversed. Dorimant's position, that vice is the exclusive pastime of the leisure class, is countered by the shoemaker's assertion that vice is a leveler, that in their failings at least all men are equal. The conclusion suggested is that to which Rochester comes in *A Satyr against Mankind:* that animal nature alone is reliable. Yet even this is one among many conclusions, for no conclusion is absolute. The system of balances that weighs fop against rake, hellion against coquette, laborer against gentleman is an end in itself. It is designed to raise issues which the play leaves unanswered. Etherege's comedies are not self-contained; there is no resolution in the end-scene marriage or betrothal of hero and heroine. Rather, the plays are constructed in the same way, to the same end, as Dryden's essays (the *Essay of Dramatic Poesy* is a good example)— to implant questions in the mind of the reader to be mused over at leisure. Complexity and contradiction are not devices in the hands of Etherege, but are the end toward which his plays strive in their effort to recreate the net of contradiction that is the human condition.

Congreve's aim is as different from the Pyrrhonistic speculation of Etherege as it is from the often brutal satire of Wycherley. He neither invites us to cool philosophical speculation nor drives us to a confrontation of human bestiality. Rather, he is concerned to excite admiration for human virtues as they are displayed in an ideal couple. In contrasting his comedy with that of his contemporaries we become aware of the strong foothold the sentimental tradition had already established by the end of the seventeenth century. The relationship of Congreve's hero and heroine is sentimental. Their virtues are good nature as well as sparkling wit. Moreover, not only are Congreve's heroes free from any suggestion of libertine malice, but even his fools are good-natured. For this reason his comedy was thought by some to defeat the didactic purpose of comedy, which requires that folly be made hateful or ridiculous upon the stage. He defended himself against this objection in his dedication to *The Way of the World:*

> Those Characters which are meant to be ridiculous in most of our Comedies, are of Fools so gross, that, in my humble Opinion, they shou'd rather disturb than divert the well-natur'd and reflecting Part of an Audience; they are rather Objects of Charity than Contempt; and instead of moving our Mirth, they ought very often to excite our Compassion.[1]

If Bergson is right in proposing that laughter has no greater foe than emotion, we can appreciate the wit and stylistic brilliance that were required to preserve Congreve's plays from degenerating into "tearful" comedy.

Congreve's method is twofold: to achieve, through subtle stylistic modulation, the distinction between true and false wit (used to display the hero and heroine like gems in a setting of inferior wits who are themselves not really fools), and to discover through the action and through character disclosure, rather than development, the "good nature," the sentimental goodness of heart, that lies beneath the brilliantly witty manners of hero and heroine. There is no conflict of interest here, as there is in Etherege; both the hero and the heroine strive toward marriage, the sentimental

1. Dedication to *The Way of the World,* in *The Complete Works of William Congreve,* ed. Montague Summers (London, 1923), *3*, 9. All references to Congreve are to this edition.

ideal. The love-chase, as it appears in Etherege, would be out of place in Congreve. The intentions of a Congreve hero are completely honorable. He loves the heroine alone, and the sole business of his life is to get her to marry him. The heroine loves the hero in return, but she tries half-heartedly to hide her feeling from him, either to test his love, as in *Love for Love,* or to play at being chased, as in *The Way of the World* (this kind of play has serious over-tones and has to do with the "Danger" of medieval romance allegory; it is the hesitance of woman to submit even to the faithful lover). Thus the love-chase of Etherege, wherein the lovers are really adversaries and there is considerable hostility in their feeling for one another, becomes in Congreve the love-game, wherein the lovers are quite obviously of one mind, are sentimentally attached, and are merely playing at having a difference of opinion. The "proviso" scene in *The Way of the World,* which many critics (includ-ing the usually perceptive Underwood) have offered as evidence of a difference in perception between hero and heroine, is a hoax. Mirabell and Millamant are in complete agreement. First of all, the professed purpose of the provi-sions is to ensure a happy life *after* marriage; there is no question in the mind of either participant about the value of marriage itself. Moreover, each knows before he states his provision that what he pretends to be guarding against is not in the nature of the other to do. Thus Millamant knows quite well that a man of Mirabell's wit would not call her names "as Wife, Spouse, My dear, Joy, Jewel . . . and the rest of that nauseous cant." In making such a proviso, she is merely displaying her own wit. Nor does she object to any of Mirabell's provisos; indeed she mocks them. *"I go to play in a mask!" "I toast Fellows! Odious men. I hate your odious provisos!"* Her reaction to the mention of "breeding" —"Ah, name it not"—makes obvious the coy pose that she has been assuming throughout the mock argument. Like all

her poses, it is transparent, an obvious mask which we watch
her take up and then discard in the spirit of the game she
plays. We are always aware that the mask is a mask and
that the hero's or heroine's object in assuming it is harmless.
Their affectations are merely one manifestation of their
cleverness, for Congreve keeps us aware always of their
fundamental good nature. There is never any confusion, as
there is in Etherege, about what is real and what false,
about where true nature ends and the disguise begins. Nor
does disguise serve Congreve's characters, as it does Wycherley's, as a means to conceal spiritual deformity or vicious
motive.

To realize his comic vision, Congreve employs traditional
plot using the sequential linear movement to unfold the
good nature of his principal characters. His commitment to
good nature, in fact, led him astray of his professed purpose
in *Love for Love*. In this play he proposed to write satire,

> Since the Plain Dealer's scenes of Manly rage
> Not one has dared to lash this crying age
> This time the poet owns the bold Essay,
>
> [Prologue]

But his central interest and romantic bent made it impossible
for him to follow in the footsteps of the Plain Dealer. From
time to time he permits his hero, Valentine, to rail mildly
at the sins of the age. For instance, pretending to be mad,
Valentine says his is the voice of Truth, and in two or three
short snatches of dialogue Congreve plays at imitating the
satiric style.

> FORESIGHT: Pray what will be done in the City?
> VALENTINE: Oh, prayers will be said in empty
> churches, at the usual hours. Yet you will see zealous
> faces behind counters as if Religion were to be sold
> in every shop. . . . And the cropt Prentice that sweeps

his Master's shop in the Morning, may, ten to one,
dirty his sheets before night. . . .   [IV, i]

But the railing, which to begin with is too mild by half, is
never supported in the scene presented us. Valentine's words
float disembodied on the surface of the play; they are never
proven in the action. Valentine's condition is eminently
suitable for a satiric spokesman; a man down on his luck
whose fair-weather friends have deserted him, whose father
hates him, whose beloved seems to scorn him, could be a
perfect malcontent satirist. But Valentine is not this; he is
exactly as his name suggests, a romantic lover. Congreve's
attention is quickly diverted from the sins of his "crying age"
to the sentimental attachment of Valentine and Angelica.
Valentine, the romantic hero, is not embittered but ennobled
by his circumstances. His noble goodness of heart is the
center of interest from the opening scenes. In the first act,
starving and harassed by duns, he is yet dismayed that his
servant should lie to his creditors. "And how the devil do
you mean to keep your word?" he asks. Although he blusters
for the instant when a former mistress who has borne him
a child comes to ask him for money, he not only gives her
the money but acknowledges that his past actions were dishonorable: "Pox on her, could she find no other time to
fling my sins in my face? Here, give her this (Gives money)."
It would be inconsistent for a Dorimant to give his last
penny to a cast mistress; it would be inconceivable for a
Horner to feel contrite about his sexual conquests.

The whole action of the play is designed to exhibit the
goodness of Valentine. He has lost his money, we learn,
through excessive generosity in love and friendship. But,
despite prodding from Jeremy, his servant, he is neither
embittered by his loss of fortune nor deterred from his
romantic quest. Rather financial ruin spurs him to new
excesses of romantic fervor.

> I'll pursue Angelica with more love than ever, and
> appear more notoriously her admirer in this restraint
> than when I openly rival'd the rich Fops that made
> court to her, so shall my poverty be a Mortification
> to her Pride, and perhaps make her Compassionate
> that Love which has principally reduced me to this
> lowness of Fortune.   [I, i]

If Valentine is the sentimental lover par excellence in his
speech, he is no less so in his actions. The plot of *Love for
Love* concerns the hero's promise to his father (the prototype
black villain of melodrama) to sign away his inheritance.
He makes the promise to obtain ready money in order that
he may honorably discharge his debts. To delay signing
away his inheritance as he had promised, Valentine pretends madness. He is led to this deception by his overpower-
ing desire to bring a fortune to the feet of Angelica. This,
with every other of his actions, is designed to the end of
winning her in marriage. Angelica tests Valentine's love by
pretending indifference to the last moment of truth. When
Valentine is pretending madness, her mask slips long enough
to reveal her love of the hero to the audience, while it is
kept secret from Valentine. The final and supreme test to
which Angelica subjects her hero's love is to pretend that
she will marry his father and thereby do him out of his
inheritance altogether. Valentine's reaction, contrary to the
fury that would seize a libertine or a malcontent satirist,
is perfectly in the sentimental strain. If he cannot have Angelica, he will gladly resign his all.

> SCANDAL: S'death! You are not mad indeed to ruin
> yourself?
> VALENTINE: I have been disappointed of my only
> hope and he that loses Hope may part with anything.
> I never valued Fortune but as it was subservient to my
> Pleasure, and my only Pleasure was to please this lady.

I have made many vain attempts and find at last that
nothing but my Ruine can effect it. Which for that
Reason I will sign to—Give me the paper.   [V, i]

Having gauged the full depth of the hero's love, Angelica
discloses her own, "I have done dissembling now, Valentine,"
and the sentimental match is made.

The same method of character disclosure is used by Congreve in *The Way of the World* to reveal the good nature of
Mirabell and Millamant. Here the heroine is more openly
in love with the hero—she is party to his plan to win her in
marriage—and her coy desire to be "solicited to the last, nay,
and afterwards," is recognized by the hero as a charming
affectation. In this play the classical formula of outwitting
senex is employed. Mirabell and Millamant together must
win over Millamant's guardian, Lady Wishfort. The plot is
so well-known that there is hardly any need to recount it.
We might simply take note of its differences from Etherege's
comedy and Wycherley's satire. There is, as we have noted,
no discord between hero and heroine. Whatever licentiousness the hero has been guilty of (his relation to Mrs. Fainall)
is past and is testimony to his honor (Mirabell has protected
Mrs. Fainall's fortune). The fools, Lady Wishfort, Willful,
and Petulant, though they are not admirable, as the hero and
heroine are, are yet good-natured fools. Their follies are
never so gross as to distort their humanity (as in Wycherley),
and the laughter they arouse is not disdainful (as in Etherege)
but is rather a mirth well-tempered with affection. Moreover,
there is no confusion, as in Etherege, about who the good
and who the bad characters are. In this respect Congreve is
well on his way to sentimental comedy. His heroes are models
of virtue, his fools are lovable eccentrics, and his villains,
Fainall and Mrs. Marwood, are so melodramatic in their
evil that one expects of them a final "Curses, foiled again!"
Fainall is, indeed, the only representative in Congreve of

the libertine view. In a few short years the libertine has
fallen from the most complex of heroes to the simplest of
villains.

Congreve's style, which reaches perfection in *The Way of
the World,* is used to three ends: to preserve the tone from
slipping into overt sentimentalism (as it does occasionally in
Love for Love), to distinguish true from false wit (which
with every other element in the play distinguishes and ideal-
izes the hero and heroine), and, finally, to achieve in art the
effect produced by conversation of men of the first wit.

When we contrast Congreve with Etherege, then, we find
that the former is by no means bringing to perfection a mode
of comedy originated by the latter. Quite the contrary, the
two playwrights worked in traditions not merely different
from, but almost inimical to each other.

Wycherley's drama distinguishes yet a third tradition.
Though he draws upon the world of multiple appearances
as well as upon the ideal world, he uses his material to ends
quite different from those of his contemporaries. Like
Etherege, he is concerned with the world as it is, with the
question of what is true and what false in human character.
But his attitude is not the detached speculative curiosity of
the skeptic. As a satirist he cannot afford moral ambivalence.

> It is notable that the satirist always operates most
> comfortably in a limited context, a rigorously circum-
> scribed world. His chosen battleground is an exact,
> literal and uncomplicated here and now. For him virtue
> is virtue and vice is vice and he carefully avoids any
> speculations about human complexity or the mysteri-
> ous nature of the universe.[2]

I would amend this definition in one respect. The satirist's
battleground is indeed here and now, but his very point is

2. Alvin Kernan, *The Cankered Muse* (New Haven, 1959), p. 244.

that reality, because it is vice-ridden, is not "uncomplicated."
In the satirist's eyes virtue is uncomplicated, truth is simple,
honesty is obvious. On the other hand, vice is complex. It
resorts to duplicity, complication, and distortion in its efforts
to cloud the distinction between good and evil, true and
false. Wycherley, then, must be as concerned as Etherege
with the world of illusion and delusion, but false appearance
interests him not in itself but as it shows how far human life
deviates from what it should be.

Wycherley touches, too, upon Congreve's world. His conception of the ideal—from his first play, where it dominates
the moral atmosphere, to his last, where it exists as an
anachronistic reminder of a past golden age—is romantic.
Unlike Congreve, however, he does not consider human
nature the embodiment of the romantic ideal. His characters
have perverted their humanity. They are goats, apes, and
asses, and they move in an atmosphere of general moral
decay. Against their corruption the ideal characters, weak
remainders of an all but lost virtue, are ineffectual. Indeed,
in Wycherley's world virtue must strive against vice constantly to exist at all.

Wycherley's focus, then, is neither upon the ideal world
nor upon the world of false appearance, but is rather upon
the difference between them. His method, the traditional
method of the satirist, is to present to our eyes a scene of
moral corruption. The love-chase plays no part in his design,
because there is neither a hero nor an ideal couple who claim
our attention. Because the satirist's interest is vice itself, it
is the scene of vice in action rather than any particular
character in it that he must illuminate. Various figures in
various relation to one another take the center of the stage
for an instant, but once their actions have proven the satiric
point, they relinquish the central position to new figures so
that a new face of the vice under consideration can be explored. When the satirist, having painted for us a vision

of universal corruption and bestiality, has completed his indictment of human nature, he then provides, to complete his satiric design, some small touchstone of virtue, the standard upon which we are to measure the deviation of human beings from humanness. In *The Country Wife* Wycherley gives us Alithea (Truth), who resists the falsity that a corrupt society forces upon her and, against all easy logic, keeps her troth, and Harcourt, her romantic lover, who wins her in honorable love after he has been made to value truth. In *The Plain Dealer,* as the scene before us is more obscene, more animal, so the ideal is more romantic and unreal. Fidelia is Wycherley's symbol of the virtue of a past age to which the satirist always looks with longing.

There is no place in this design for a hero. Those characters of Wycherley who have been mistaken for heroes, Manly and Horner, are satiric spokesmen. Drawing upon an Elizabethan convention, Wycherley uses a satiric spokesman who, though he draws our attention to the vice and hypocrisy before us, yet illustrates it in his own nature as well. Horner, for instance, clearly sees lust leering beneath the carefully maintained façade of the honorable ladies, Fidget, Squeamish, and company. He exposes their lust and their hypocrisy to the audience, and in the tradition of the parasite-satirist, he exploits it. But he himself is the most outrageous example of vice masquerading as innocence that the play affords. He stands out in the play not as a hero but as an exaggeration, an emblem of the vice in question. In the same way Manly, the plain dealer, rails against the falsity and diseased sexuality of the age. But he becomes a double dealer when he disguises his own lust as a desire for honorable revenge and his own exploitation as honorable friendship. He proves himself to be at last one of the very company that disgusts him.

Wycherley's style is the harsh tone of the satirist; his wit is the biting, cruel wit of a Juvenal. It is used to strip the painted surface of false convention, to flay the pious face of the hypocrite. There are no heroes, no heroines, no lovable fools in Wycherley; there are only knaves and gulls who are themselves would-be knaves and, in a corner of the satiric scene, solitary examples of virtue. In this atmosphere of dishonest knaves and libidinous bitches, the sentimentality of Congreve's lovers, the devilish charm of Etherege's rakes and flirtatious coquettes, would wither. Compare, for example, Lady Wishfort's affectations as she attempts to disguise her "green-sickness" with Lady Fidget's calculated "honor." Congreve's old fool is comic; she arouses our affection as well as mirth. Wycherley's lady calls forth a sardonic grin and, at last, disgusts us. Olivia of *The Plain Dealer* actually shocks us, she is so like a mean-tempered bitch in heat.

If we brought our comparison of the three dramatists no further than their "comic heroes," of whom so much has been said, we would be forced to conclude that the differences between the three are more important than their similarities. Etherege's hero has strong affiliations with the heroic drama. He is the constant object of our admiration, because his wit and charm, as well as his malice and depravity, are so prodigious that they fill us with a kind of wonder and throw about his actions an aura of glamour. We identify with this hero, and we are, for a moment lifted out of ourselves. Here the Freudian theory applies. We like Etherege's hero because he is bold enough to break the rules of conduct that we would like to break. He is the hero of our private selves. Congreve's hero is the hero of our public selves. He, too, arouses admiration, but it is exactly opposite to the kind that Etherege's hero excites. We like Congreve's hero not because he breaks moral convention but because he embodies it and makes it attractive, because he possesses in perfection those qualities that we should like to think we exhibit to the world, a good heart and a brilliant wit. It is quite significant that Congreve's hero shares his spotlight with a heroine (in Etherege the heroine is merely a foil for the hero), because the virtues he possesses are feminine. He is not special because of his sexual prowess or heroic malice but for tenderness of heart and wit that is sharp but not cruel. Wycherley's "heroes" are not heroes but satiric spokesmen. They only seem for a moment to be better than the hypocrites whom they attack. But they, too, are at last unmasked. No special virtue distinguishes them from the other figures in the scene of vice and hypocrisy, because in satire the scene, not the figures in it, is paramount. Wycherley uses the satiric spokesman to show the difference between our public and private selves, to unmask what we pretend to be and reveal what we are, to show how far what we are deviates from what we should be. The private self of Wycherley's satiric spokesman has nothing of the grand manner of an Etheregean libertine. In Wycherley vice is mean, petty, ugly; the spokesman's depravity is either faintly disgusting, as in Horner, or brutally shocking and diseased as in Manly.

This brings us to the final point of our comparison, the difference between obscenity and immorality and the functions of these in the drama we have been discussing. In Etherege the immoral is not obscene—that is, it does not disgust. It represents one view of life that the play attempts to investigate. But since it represents the hero's point of view, the admiration we feel for him colors our perception of the immoral, enhances and glamourizes it. Therefore, if we were to view Etherege's comedy from the position of a seventeenth- or eighteenth-century critic, who would consider that the purpose of comedy is to instruct by rendering what is immoral ridiculous, we should have to concede that Etherege's works are immoral. If, however, we consider them in the light of a more recent critical view, we might argue that since the admiration of the immoral that is aroused by the plays is also dissipated by them as we, so to speak, live out our immoral urges vicariously through the hero, the plays are, after all, not immoral. They purge us of our own desire for the immoral life.

In Congreve there is neither immorality nor obscenity. Whatever indecency there is in the plays exists purely on the verbal level, in punning and word play. If immoral action is mentioned, it is past action (Valentine's old mistress, the implied relation between Mirabell and Mrs. Fainall), which has occurred before the play begins and which is considered an error that the hero has overcome.

In Wycherley the immoral is truly obscene. This presents us with the curious paradox that is inherent in the satiric vision. Satire is moral, the most overtly moral of poetic genres, since its professed aim is to attack vice. However, since the business of satire is vice, it must show in detail the workings of immorality. It presents the immoral in all its obscenity, operating on the assumption that

> Vice is a monster of so fearful mien
> As, to be hated, needs but to be seen
> [Pope, "Essay on Man," II]

However, the detail with which he describes vice often gives us the impression that the satirist is a kind of moral pervert smacking his lips over the depravity that he sees all around him. When satire is rendered in the dramatic mode, the relation between the writer and his character, the satiric spokesman in the play, is easily confused. Since Restoration comedy has for so long been considered a perfect representation of the writer's view of his society, Wycherley's moral position has been consistently confused with that of his satiric spokesmen. Thus Wimsatt and Brooks[3] speak of "Horneresque indecency" as one of the defects from which "Res-

3. W. K. Wimsatt and Cleanth Brooks, *Literary Criticism: A Short History* (New York, 1957), p. 210.

toration comedy" suffers, ignoring not just the distinction among Restoration comedies but also the peculiarity of Horneresque indecency and the function it serves in Wycherley's plays. Wycherley uses obscenity in the same way and to the same end as Swift. His obscenity is as brutal, disgusting, and shocking as the bestial human behavior it attacks. Obscenity is the traditional handmaiden of English satire; it will be the aim of the succeeding chapters to prove that Wycherley is a master of that art.

2. Wycherley's Early Plays: the shepherd's voice

THE CANON of Wycherley's plays, meager as it is, can nevertheless be of great value to the student of literary history, for the development of his aesthetic approach reflects the revolution from Renaissance to Augustan aesthetics and establishes the Restoration period as the critical pivot upon which the change occurs. Wycherley's first play, *Love in a Wood,* despite its setting in St. James's park and liberal topical allusion, is Elizabethan in conception. Analysis reveals it to be a close imitation of Fletcher's *The Faithful Shepherdess.* Yet interesting as this is in itself, Wycherley's source is of minor significance compared with his choice of the pastoral form and his method of imitation, for in these latter he shows his adherence to Elizabethan principles. In his second play, *The Gentleman Dancing Master,* a hastily wrought farce that fails artistically, he wavers between Jonsonian "humour" and Restoration wit but the very crudity of his artistry reveals his method of approach. In his best achievements, *The Country Wife* and *The Plain Dealer,* each a perfectly wrought formal satire, not only do the two major streams of the English satiric tradition converge, but two methods of imitation—the Renaissance and the new Restoration approaches to ancient literature—are clearly evident.

The state of Restoration satire is roughly comparable to what occurs in language. Just as we have neologisms directly coined from Latin and older Anglo-Latin words originally derived from Latin but amended by the native linguistic tradition, so we have in Restoration satire a direct and fresh perception of ancient satire as well as a satiric inheritance from the Elizabethan period that is an amalgam of ancient English and bastardized Latin elements. In form Wycherley's mature plays indicate the Restoration's new approach to ancient models, a method of imitation that stresses architectural structure. In characterization of the satiric spokesman, he shows his dependence upon Elizabethan satiric decorum. His is the Elizabethan conception of the satyr-satirist, the end product of a native English tradition that was shaped by Renaissance methods of imitation.

The literary growth of the age, then, out of an Elizabethan past toward the development of a new aesthetic, is reflected in the literary development of Wycherley himself. Curiously enough, the transition is from that genre most typical of the Renaissance, pastoral, to that most typical of the Augustan mode, satire—but these are, after all, but opposite sides of the same coin. In tracing the origins of the tragi-comic pattern, E. M. Waith, in a chapter entitled "Satyr and Shepherd" explores the oddly inextricable relationship that exists between these two figures and the genres they represent. Critics of pastoral from Greg to Empson agree that the universal essential in this mode is the contrast, stated or implied, between the ideal life of the good shepherd and the imperfect world of reality. "In pastoral literature . . . a longing for the ideal existence symbolized by the pastoral life exists side by side with the portrayal in Arcadia of conditions obviously similar to those of corrupt Italy or England."[1] Cast upon the idyllic world of romance is the shadow of the satyr, from Guarini's Corisca to D'Urfé's Hylas to Fletcher's Sullen Shepherd and Shakespeare's Jaques.

1. E. M. Waith, *The Pattern of Tragi-Comedy in Beaumont and Fletcher* (New Haven, 1952), p. 71; cf. W. W. Greg, *Pastoral Poetry and Pastoral Drama* (New York, 1959), p. 4.

The satyr need not appear with cloven foot and hairy leg, but the irregularity of his nature must be represented in some figure who, in his defiance of the ideal world or in his moral deformity, stands as the reminder of the dark side of life, of corrupt reality. Similarly, satire bears as its core a contrast between the vision of corruption it presents and the ideal existence, usually some golden lost age of innocence, for which it longs. "The satirist who portrays with awful vividness the very conditions from which the pastoral poet longs to escape, occasionally uses the simple country life as an antithesis to the corruption he satirizes."[2] Juvenal, in his *Eleventh Satire,* invites a friend to a country-style dinner. As he describes the simple hearty food, the plain service, the humble courtesy of the country boys who will serve, he draws a contrast between the good life of the country and the enervating luxury of Rome (and, incidentally, reinforces the contrast between what Romans should be, what they were in a lost noble age, and what they have become). With consummate skill Horace (*Satire VI, II*) uses an idyllic morning (1–23) and evening (60–76) in the country to set off his central picture of a feverish day in Rome (23–59) and emblemizes his contrast in the closing allegory of the city mouse and the country mouse. With like sophistication, the mature Wycherley sets off the diseased atmosphere of *The Plain Dealer* with the figure of Fidelia, an image straight out of the green world of Elizabethan romantic comedy.

The further we investigate the relationship the stronger the connection between these genres appears to be. Most of the greatest satirists tried their hands at pastoral, Pope in his first ventures, Dryden in his translations. "Somehow the satirist seems always to come from a world of pastoral innocence and kindness; he is the prophet come down from the hills to the cities of the plain ... abroad in the cruel world."[3]

2. Waith, p. 71.
3. Kernan, *The Cankered Muse,* p. 18.

The very polarity of good and evil in the black–white vision
that satire demands implies the idealized world of pastoral
as the yearned-after good. On the Frye continuum[4] they are
visualized as opposites, but opposites of the same degree of
intensity; the existence of the one genre demands the existence of the other. This is not to imply that the pastoral and
satiric visions must exist in separate, opposite forms. A whole
tradition in which pastoral is the vehicle for satire (from
Mantuano to Spenser's *Shepheard's Calender*), or where satire
takes the form of burlesque pastoral (*The Beggar's Opera*)
testifies to the closeness with which they may adhere. Satire
and pastoral are opposite manifestations of the same sensibility, two prospects from the same vantage point. Waith
catches the difference in perspective in a neat figure: ". . . The
meaning of pastoral romance depends upon sharing the feelings of St. George as he tackles the dragon. In the meaning
of satire, however, St. George is almost overlooked while
we are asked to stand outside and consider the menace of
the dragon."[5] Wycherley's progress as a playwright describes
this shift in perspective from pastoral to satire. His first
play is a Restoration rendition of pastoral. Satire appears
only as an element in the pastoral scheme. As he develops
in his art satire overwhelms romance until, in the last play,
romance is merely an element in the satiric design.

It is little wonder that Wycherley's first play should be a
pastoral that imitates Fletcher in over-all pattern and draws
heavily upon Jonson for elements within the Fletcherian
design. Beaumont and Fletcher, Jonson, and Shakespeare
were the darlings of the restored theatre. It is impossible to
exaggerate their impact, especially that of the first three,
upon the period.[6] During the first season, 1660–61, in less

4. Northrop Frye, *Anatomy of Criticism* (Princeton, 1957).
5. Waith, pp. 84–85.
6. Cf. A. C. Sprague, *Beaumont and Fletcher on the Restoration Stage*
    (Cambridge, Mass., 1926); J. H. Wilson, *The Influence of Beaumont*

than nine months of acting time nearly half the plays presented were those of Beaumont and Fletcher. The briefest
perusal of the play lists from 1660 to the turn of the century
shows clearly that the plays of the triumvirate formed the
basic repertory, with Beaumont and Fletcher in the lead,
followed by Jonson and then Shakespeare. Legal provisions
were drawn up by the two companies shortly after their
formation ensuring the rights of each to certain of the Beaumont and Fletcher plays and certain of Jonson's comedies,
for it was recognized that either company's holding a mo-
nopoly upon them could destroy the other.

The admiration accorded the three was not merely blanket
praise. Critics of the period carefully differentiated among
them, according each praise for his particular excellence.
Shakespeare was prized for his "natural wit" (hence his
position at the bottom of the list), Jonson for his learning
and his knowledge of human nature, particularly of the
excesses of human nature. Fletcher was esteemed for the
luxury of his invention and his polished courtly style, but
most of all for the touches of passion in his graceful handling
of romantic love. Throughout the period critics—Dryden,
Phillips, Winstanley, Blount—repeat the well-known formula:

> each excelled in his particular way; Ben Jonson in his
> elaborate pains and knowledge of authors, Shakespeare
> in his pure vein of wit and natural poetic height,
> Fletcher in his courtly elegance and gentle familiarity
> of style and withal a wit and invention so overflowing
> that the luxuriant branches thereof were frequently
> thought convenient to be lopt off by Mr. Beaumont.[7]

---

and Fletcher on Restoration Drama (Columbus, 1928); and R. G.
Noyes, Ben Jonson on the English Stage, 1660–1776 (Cambridge,
Mass., 1935).

7. Thomas Blount, De Re Poetica (1694), as quoted in Wilson, p. 15.

The influence of Beaumont and Fletcher reigned supreme because the foundation of Restoration taste was laid in the pastoral-mad Caroline period, when they were almost the only English playwrights of an earlier age who were admired. The greatest patron of the restored theatre, the king, was twelve when the playhouses were closed in 1642, and he was the son of a queen who had decided tastes in drama. The courtly audience as well as some of the major playwrights had just returned from France, the birthplace of *L'Astrée* and the romances of La Calprenède and de Scudéry. Wycherley himself had spent the period of exile in close proximity to the salon of Julie D'Argennes, the eldest daughter of the Marquise de Rambouillet and the last of the great précieuses. At the opening of the theatres in 1660 those hardy survivors of the Interregnum, Davenant and Killigrew, picked up where they had been interrupted, drawing upon the labyrinthine pastorals of Rutter, Cowley, and Digby. *The Faithful Shepherdess* was among the first plays to be revived, for though a failure when it was first produced in 1608, it had enjoyed smashing success when revived for the pleasure of the Caroline court in 1635. The Fletcherian technique of separable scenes had also made parts of his plays suitable for presentation as drolls during the Interregnum. In the early days of the restored theatre, then, loosely structured romance was the dominant form, romantic love the proper subject, and courtly elegance the proper style of comedy. Fletcher's star dominated the horizon.

Jonson, esteemed as he was, was not the poet to whom a writer in search of subject or design would go. Even his greatest admirer was careful to circumscribe the limits of his art:

> But let us not think him a perfect pattern for imitation except it be in humour; for love, which is the foundation of all comedies in other languages, is scarcely mentioned

in any of his comedies; and for humour itself, the poets of this age will be more wary than to imitate the meanness of his persons. Gentlemen will now be entertained with the follies of each other, and though they allow Cobb and Tib to speake properly, yet they are not much pleased with their tankard or with their rags.[8]

However, if he was not to be looked to as a model in the composition of romantic comedy, he was nevertheless the acknowledged master of, and model for, "humour." The knowledge of human nature for which he is everywhere praised is the knowledge of human nature in all its corruption. Humour is the delineation to grotesquely exaggerated effect of the excesses, the distorting defects, in human nature. Jonson's characterization, exaggerating downward in exact opposition to the idealizing vision of romance, provides the figure of the satyr essential in the pastoral scheme, the reminder that corrupt reality exists.

Wycherley goes first to Fletcher, from whom he borrows for his first play the loosely constructed pastoral framework. The central concern of the pastoral drama of the seventeenth century is the presentation of an ideal of love, and the triumph of that ideal over those other kinds of love that represent varying degrees of deviation from the ideal. The ideal is embodied in a woman (in this period pastoral is decidedly feministic in tone) and is Platonic in nature. The lover of the ideal woman, though not as perfect as she, comes closest to her in perfection, and their love is heroic. However, essential to the pastoral scheme are gradations of love, from supersensuous idealism to bestiality. If the ideal couple stand at the topmost point in the scale of love, they have a counterpart, morally deformed, who stands at the bottom—the satyr in the landscape. Between these extremes are other figures,

8. Dryden, "Defense of the Epilogue," *Works,* ed. Sir Walter Scott and George Saintsbury (18 vols. Edinburgh, 1882–92), 4, 242.

each representing a degree of love. In Greg's definition, "the characters fall into certain distinct groups which may be regarded as exemplifying certain aspects of love. Supersensuous sentiment . . . chaste and honorable regard . . . natural and unrestrained desire and violent lust."[9] To accommodate this scheme of a hierarchy of love, the plot of pastoral romance consists in the weaving together of multiple courtships. Confusion and suspense are added, to loosen the plot and thus avoid a too stately pairing, by the use of such traditionally romantic devices as disguise and mistaken identity. The business of most of the characters in pastoral is to enact or to discuss questions of love—the pseudo-problems of the Renaissance, Italian courtly tradition, such as, the value of absence from the beloved, the uses of jealousy, etc. These discussions, conducted in courtly diction and deadly earnest by the high characters are parodied in the conversation of the low characters,[1] for the differentiation of characters into high, medium, and low is reflected in the style of their discourse. High characters speak a floridly romantic, heroic diction; middle characters converse at the level of discourse common to the age in which the work was written; and low characters use the style of Cobb and Tib. In some works it is possible to gauge the worth of a character on the instant of his first appearance by whether he speaks in verse or prose. The sprawling design of this kind of drama is subject to no further discipline than the final gathering together of characters for a resolution of the central mystery, a re-establishment of real identities and a cleansing of the morally impure (generally through the good offices or example of the ideal woman) before the end-scene multiple wedding.

9. Greg, p. 269. This gradation of love can be observed in Guarini, in D'Urfé, and even in *As You Like It.*
1. We can observe this in even so early an English romance as Sidney's *Arcadia,* where the conversations of Philoclea and Pyrocles are parodied in the crude exchanges of Dametas and Miso.

In his choice of so loosely structured a scheme as the infinitely expandable, infinitely variable pastoral design, as well as in his methods of imitation, Wycherley at this early stage reveals a Renaissance aesthetic outlook. In this first play formal structure concerns him hardly at all. Rather he considers structure the mere framework for brilliant effects. He shows in this that he is very much of the age preceding his, an age whose aesthetic emphasized parts to the detriment of the whole architecture in a work of art.

> I value language as a conduit, the variety thereof to several shapes and adorned Truth or witty Inventions that which it should deliver. I compare a Poem to a garden ... and the variety of Invention to the Diversity of Flowers thereof . . . a grave sentence . . . a witty conceit . . . a generous rapture . . . all the rest, for the most part, is but a naked Narration or gross staff to uphold the general Frame ...[2]

This late Renaissance critic describes exactly Wycherley's conception of structure in his first play. He borrows "a generous rapture" or a "grave sentence" for his high characters from Fletcher, turns "a witty conceit" by playing upon the contrast between his middle characters—Etheregean beaux and flirts—and those found in traditional pastoral, peoples his "low" plane with Puritan humour characters straight out of Jonson's *Bartholomew Fair*. His art is displayed in the immediate effect, in the brilliance of a turn of wit. As for the structure of the whole, that is merely "a naked Narration," an obvious device to hold the pastoral circus together. The method of imitation demanded by such a conception, too, is of the Renaissance. As Jonson says, "One though he be excellent and the chief is not to be imitated alone." Critics from Vida and Minturno to their English disciples of the

---

2. William Alexander, *Anacrises* (1634), in *Critical Essays of the Seventeenth Century* ed. J. E. Spingarn (3 vols. Oxford, 1908), *I*, 182.

Elizabethan age stress the borrowing of bits and snatches, stylistic devices, figures. One encounters again and again in Renaissance Italian and Elizabethan criticism the image of one imitator going from model to model "to draw forth out of the best and choicest flowers, with the bee, and turn all into honey, worke it into one relish and savour; make our imitation sweet."[3] Wycherley borrows freely from Fletcher and Jonson, blending their effects with his own in the witty mélange of a Restoration pastoral.

His most brilliant effect is rendering so stiffly artificial a series of tableaux as Fletcher's *Faithful Shepherdess* into Restoration terms. Fletcher's play, regarded by Greg as the finest English example of the pastoral drama, is a perfect fulfillment of the hierarchic scheme of love outlined above. Clorin, who gives the play its name, has at the opening just buried her beloved. So pure and free from fleshly concerns is her love, however, that it lives on unchanged, though he is dead. She vows that she will be wedded to his memory, that she will retire from even the innocent joys of the pastoral life:

> No more the company of fresh fair maids
> And wanton shepherds be to me delightful.[4]

She determines to spend the rest of her days beside his grave, practicing the use of herbs. Besides being pledged to an ideal love, Clorin by virtue of her virginity is possessed of magic power. Her chastity enables her to tame the savage, to cure physical ills, and to purge spiritual impurity.

After Clorin in virtue comes Amoret, the beloved of the shepherd Perigot. This couple, too, is united in a pure Platonic love. Perigot is slightly less perfect in his love than

3. Ben Jonson, *Timber, or Discoveries,* ed. I. Gollancz (London, 1898), p. 119.
4. All references to Fletcher are to *The Works of Beaumont and Fletcher,* ed. H. Weber (14 vols. Edinburgh, 1812).

Amoret, however, because he does not have absolute faith
in her purity, though admittedly the test of his faith is severe.
Amarillis, a shepherdess vainly in love with Perigot, is transformed into the exact image of Amoret. In this disguise she
intercepts Perigot, who at midnight is on his way to a wood
where he and Amoret are to plight their troth. Amarillis
tries to seduce Perigot. He is enraged by the apparent fall
from virtue of his beloved. Having turned Perigot against
Amoret, Amarillis goes off and resumes her natural shape.
Meanwhile the real Amoret arrives at the designated meeting
place, where the incensed Perigot stabs her. Amoret's love
for him is, of course, not a jot diminished by his apparently
unreasonable assault. She is rescued by a river god because
she is a virgin, is stabbed once again by Perigot, and finally
is healed by Clorin.

Next in the chain of love is Amarillis, who is much less
pure than Amoret and Perigot. Not above ignoble action to
satisfy her amorous desires, as we have seen, Amarillis is
yet capable of reformation. Amarillis makes a bargain with
the Sullen Shepherd, the evil genius of the play, to submit
to his lust if he will help her to win Perigot's love. It is the
Sullen Shepherd who transforms her into the image of
Amoret. However, once the bargain is made, Amarillis
repents it and flees in terror from the Sullen Shepherd's
raging sexuality. The male counterpart of Amarillis is Alexis,
a wanton shepherd. He, too, is tainted with carnal passion
but is amenable to reform.

Near the bottom of the scale, before the absolute nadir of
the vice-ridden Sullen Shepherd, we come upon Cloe, the
wanton shepherdess. Cloe spends most of her time wandering
through the woods actively courting assault. During the day
she disguises her diseased sexuality and, pretending that she,
like the other Arcadians, is Platonically in love, she makes
seemingly innocent assignations with two different shepherds. This is merely her device for luring them into the

forest, where she fervently hopes one or the other of them will seduce her—so wild is her appetite that it makes no distinction between them. When both of them fail her, one because he is virtuous and the other because he is wounded by the Sullen Shepherd, the nymphomaniacal Cloe ranges through the forest in search of other prospects. She fears only wild beasts, she declares; men cannot terrify her because "I cannot be raped / I am so willing."

The Sullen Shepherd, so morally deformed that he is almost bestial, is the satyr figure in the pastoral landscape. His very being itself is inimical to the ideal world presided over by Clorin. Not only is he too far gone in vice to be cured by her, but he emanates an evil power of his own. If he so much as approaches Clorin's grove, her magic is rendered ineffectual. At the approach of the satyr, the symbol of corrupt reality, the whole airy, fragile vision of pastoral romance threatens to dissolve.

At the end of the play those who can be are cured by Clorin, the Sullen Shephed is banished, and the couples are united by the priest of Pan.

> In speeches as formal as the movement of a dancer they exhibit their diverse natures and establish the themes of the play. Then follows a series of regroupings—variations on the opening themes—continuing to the end of the last act. The plot, like the story of a ballet, is less important than the component situations in which an idea, a relationship, or an emotion is given a brief, vivid actuality.[5]

Being so variable and therefore so perfect a display case for effects, this play exactly suited Wycherley's purposes. His most artful among many brilliant effects was to play upon the familiar Fletcher plot, rendering it in modern terms, yet

5. Waith, p. 5.

in the very process to preserve its original pastoral intention.

To transfer the meadows and forests of Arcadia to the midst of Restoration London, to make the pastoral "wood" of *Love in a Wood* St. James's Park, is so delightfully absurd that it skirts parody. Yet the wood serves in earnest the function of the pastoral wood. It reduces men to essence.

> DAP: [Here] a man of wit may have the better of the dumb show of well-trimmed vest or fair peruke:—no man's now is whitest.
> RAN: And now no woman's modest or proud; for her blushes are hid, and the rubies on her lips are dyed, and all sleepy and glimmering eyes have lost their attraction.
> VN: ... and no observing spruce fop will miss the cravat that lies on one's shoulder, or count the pimples on one's face.   [II, i]

As the pastoral wood must, the park serves as the scene of the initial confusion of identities as well as the place where the final resolution occurs. In the wood the chaste and virtuous will be distinguished from the bestial, and the hypocritical will be unmasked. Peopled with characters who, despite their Restoration names, represent heroic love, natural love, lust, etc., the park reveals that in intention as well as design, *Love in a Wood* is pastoral romance.

Wycherley's scale of love, in close imitation of Fletcher, stretches from the highly romantic attachment of Christina and Valentine, through the more realistic love-chase of Ranger and Lydia, to the rock-bottom lechery of Alderman Gripe and the cold calculation of Lucy Crossbite, his wench. The names of the characters alone indicate their positions on the scale. At the topmost level, in the rarefied atmosphere of supersensuous sentiment and Fletcherian romantic diction, is Christina, who twice in the play is openly called "the faithful shepherdess."[6] The object of her idealized passion, Valentine, is almost but not quite worthy of her. His flaw, typical of the pastoral hero, is lack of faith in the absolute virtue of his beloved. This failing, stimulated by the usual imbroglio of disguises and mistaken identity, initiates the problems of the high plot.[7]

Less perfect in love and more realistic in diction are Ranger and Lydia. Ranger is a Restoration libertine and Lydia the female wit who snares him. As his name implies, his fault is infidelity. He loves Lydia but he chases other women, mostly for sport, since it is the game itself that intrigues him. However, by the end of the play through the good offices of the faithful shepherdess, Christina, he is made to go sighing "Lydia! Lydia!" through the wood in the best pastoral manner. Lydia exactly corresponds to Ranger in degree of perfection. She is idealized, especially in the quality of her wit, but she is not an ideal, as Christina is. Lydia is chaste and high-born but she is also witty and spirited. No faithful shepherdess she. Jealous of Ranger with reason, she decides to follow him into the park rather than wait docilely for him to come to her. While she is there she is not above engaging in wit-combat with the sparks. In Lydia, Wycherley tempered Fletcher's Amoret by incorporating Amarillis into her characterization.

The next step downward on the scale of love is, interestingly, a step down on the social scale as well. The pair at this level are hypocrites who aspire above themselves. Dapperwit, a fop and would-be wit, takes as his partner Martha, the daughter of Alderman Gripe. They are a well-matched pair of double-dealers; Dapperwit is after Martha's fortune

6. At the beginning and end of II, ii. All references are to the Mermaid Edition, *William Wycherley,* ed. W. C. Ward (London, 1888).

7. The play cannot really be said to have a high and low plot. High, medium, and low plot will be used here to signify the actions that take place on the three stylistic levels of the play.

and Martha wants a pretty witling for relief from the Puritans among whom she lives.

One rung from the bottom of the scale is Wycherley's close rendition of Fletcher's Cloe. Lady Flippant nudges her brother's servants into seducing her, relentlessly pursues Dapperwit, who she knows despises her, and hires a bawd to get her a husband. When all expedients fail, like Cloe she ranges through the park, a predatory beast: "Unfortunate lady that I am! I have left the herd on purpose to be chased, and have wandered this hour here; but the Park affords not so much as a satyr for me, and (that's strange) no Burgundy man or drunken scourer will reel my way" (V, ii). Here is the indiscriminate appetite of the nymphomaniac, but diseased as it is it has not yet reached the bottom of the scale, where carnality and greed blend to mark the satyr's imprint on the pastoral design.

At the absolute nadir, exaggerated downward to the same degree as Christina and Valentine are idealized, are the Jonsonian humour characters, Alderman Gripe, Lucy Crossbite, Mrs. Joyner. Their lechery and avarice create an impression of impenetrable materialism to counterbalance the pure essence of the ideal. In the worst among them, Gripe, materialism is distorted into more grotesque deformity by hypocrisy. "Peace, plenty, and pastime be within these walls" (III, iii) he cants upon entering the house of a wench he means to buy at the lowest possible price. Taking the precedent of Jonson's *The Sad Shepherd,* Wycherley makes his satyr figures, the lecher, the bawd, and the pimp, Puritans.

The division required by the hierarchy of love into high, middle, and low characters is correspondingly reflected in the necessity for high, middle, and low action and styles. Interestingly, these lines of demarcation also differentiate between the separate uses to which Wycherley puts his models. In the high plot Wycherley seriously imitates Fletcher. The high characters are clearly drawn after those in Fletcherian tragi-comedy. They function less as characters than as counters, abstract symbols that can be moved here or there to set a contrast or strike a pleasing arrangement. Christina, who was played by Mrs. Boutell, an actress famous for her portrayal of Aspatia in *The Maid's Tragedy,* is a mixture of Clorin and Amoret. Her lament, in properly elevated diction, for the absence of her beloved, introduces the high plot. "Unhappy Valentine! Couldst thou but see how soon thy absence and misfortunes have disbanded all thy friends, and turned thy slaves all renegadoes, thou sure wouldst prize my only faithful heart" (II, ii). We learn that before the action of the play Valentine has fought a duel in defense of Christina's honor and, having nearly killed his opponent, has been forced to flee to France. Christina, dressed in heavy mourning, has retired to spend the time of his absence weeping over his picture, having made the traditional vow of the romantic heroine: "to see the face of no man, till an unfortunate friend of mine, now out of the kingdom, return" (II, ii). The kingdom might as well be Arcadia as England. So faithful is Christina to her vow that she would not become involved in the action at all were not disguise, accident and coincidence, the devices traditionally employed to stir into motion the still-life pastoral tableaux, called into play. Lydia, modeled we will recall upon Fletcher's Amarillis, has not the perfect faith and serenity of Christina. She has gone to the park to track Ranger, but she would like to keep her identity concealed from him. When Ranger spots her and pursues her to Christina's house, she begs Christina to help her to deceive him. Conveniently, Lydia and Christina are of the same stature, and Lydia too is in mourning. Much against her will, Christina is persuaded to receive Ranger and to tell him that it is she whom he has pursued from the park. In this way Fletcher's Amoret-Amarillis confusion is introduced.

Ranger, adept at the love game, instantly fabricates the

tale that he is aware that he was pursuing Christina, that he has been adoring her from afar for weeks. Christina is, of course, properly angry and shows him out. However, Lydia, who has overheard Ranger's false protestation, believes it and decides to test his fidelity to her. She sends him a note in Christina's hand, proposing an assignation.

In the meantime Valentine has returned from France. We come upon him in the apartments of his friend Vincent discussing, in the aphoristic formulae of the Renaissance courtly lover, "pleasant questions of love."

> VAL: . . . as absence is the bane of common and bastard love, 'tis the vindication of that which is true and generous.
>
> VIN: Nay, if you could ever doubt her love, you deserve to doubt on; for there is no punishment great enough for jealousy—but jealousy. [II, iv]

Ranger, unfortunately, appears, boasting to Vincent that he has followed Christina home from the park and has fallen in love with her. Valentine, hearing him, is enraged. Like Perigot he has not that unshakable faith in the virtue of his beloved demanded by the romantic code. Even the assurance of Christina's maid that her mistress has never broken her retired solitude does not satisfy him. Rather, the conflicting testimonies of Ranger and the maid launch him upon an extended discussion with Vincent of the nature of jealousy which, as even this small excerpt demonstrates, is in the best précieux pastoral manner.

> VIN: But if both testimonies are fallible, why will you needs believe his? We are apter to believe the things we would have than those we would not.
>
> VAL: My ill luck has taught me to credit my misfortunes and doubt my happiness. . . .
>
> VIN: Will you judge of fortune by your experience, and

not do your mistress the same justice? Go see her . . .
for it she be innocent, consider how culpable you are,
not only in your censures of her, but in not seeing her
since your coming.

VAL: If she be innocent, I should be afraid to surprise
her, for her sake; if false, I should be afraid to surprise
her for my own.   [IV, v]

Ranger, receiving the note that he thinks is from Christina,
sends a messenger to escort her to Vincent's house, where
he proposes to meet her. But he first goes to Vincent's house
to boast to Valentine and Vincent of his victory over Christina's virtue. His messenger meanwhile escorts the masked
Lydia, who he thinks is Christina, to Vincent's house. Unfortunately, Christina, having been informed of Valentine's
return, chooses just this moment to seek him in Vincent's
house. When she arrives, both Valentine and Vincent think
that she has indeed come to meet Ranger. The enraged
Valentine draws his sword, and when Christina steps in
front of it to prevent him for his own good from fighting,
he thinks she is trying to defend Ranger and rushes off into
the park.

The lovers all come together in the wood, where Christina clears herself, Valentine learns to trust his mistress, and
Ranger, chastened and bewildered by Christina's coldness,
learns to value Lydia and tearfully sighs her name through
the wood. Christina, though she lacks the magic herbs of
Clorin, manages to "cure" the jealousy of Valentine, the
wantonness of Ranger, and the boldness of Lydia, by her
virtue and the example of her fidelity.

Perfect decorum of characterization, diction, and action is
not only maintained but also contained within each level.
For example, Vincent, a character who moves on two levels
—on the middle plane as one of the Restoration wits and
on the high plane as the indispensable friend of the romantic

lover—changes as he moves from one to the other level. In the company of the wits he assumes the diction of the Restoration spark ("Now a man may carry a bottle under his arm instead of a hat"), as well as the manner and action of the typically Etheregean honnête homme: "[Chasing a woman in the park] Nay, now I am sure you will stay and be kind, for coyness in a woman is as little a sign of true modesty as huffing in a man is a sign of true courage." Yet when he ascends to join Christina and Valentine on the high plane, he at once steps into the romantic stereotype that awaits him there. He is "the friend," the indispensable adviser-confidant with whom the heroic lover shares the secrets of his heart. His actions in this role are chivalrous (he defends the honor of Christina from Valentine's suspicions); his arguments and manner of presenting them are straight out of a Renaissance text; his diction is impeccably romantic: "Methinks she should be innocent; her tongue and eyes together with that flood that swells 'em do vindicate her heart" (IV, v). On the middle plane Wycherley plays upon the Fletcherian romantic style for satiric effect, yet preserves Fletcher's pastoral intention. As we have observed, the central concern of pastoral is to present the triumph of ideal love over those other kinds of love that represent varying degrees of deviation from the ideal. Therefore, love in the modern Restoration style, whether the love of rake and female wit (Ranger and Lydia) or the love of the predatory female and her cully (Lady Flippant and Sir Simon Addlepot) is a falling off, in varying degrees, from the ideal of love that the high plot presents. Wycherley's method in the middle plane is to build into the diction and actions of the characters the standard upon which we are to measure their deviation from the ideal. Because the middle-plane characters are more realistic, more nearly material beings than the shadowy abstractions of the high plot, we are apt to mistake their function, considering them merely realistic portraits of contemporary types (the rakes and wenches of the Restoration age that the playwrights are thought to portray "with photographic realism"). However, when we recognize the scheme of *Love in a Wood* as pastoral, we realize that a middle style, written at the level of discourse common to the age in which the work is written, is part of the pastoral design, and that within the pastoral scheme the middle plane represents a fall from the perfection of the high plane. Employing a clever use of allusion, Wycherley keeps before our eyes the standard of perfection at the same time as he maintains the decorum of the middle style. One of his devices is to use isolated key pastoral words in place of their contemporary equivalents, as "For now a-nights the jostling nymph is bolder/ Than modern satyr with his cloak o'er shoulder" (II, i). The incongruity of the words "nymph" and "satyr" with the image of a bold, jostling Restoration female and her becloaked dandy of a male counterpart emphasizes how far modern life is a deviation from the pastoral ideal.

The diction of the middle characters is either a confusion of pastoral allusion with Restoration slang, suggesting the moral confusion of the speaker, or a parody of the romantic diction of the high characters, indicating the degree to which the speaker deviates from the ideal. For example, Lady Flippant's wild, indiscriminate sexuality is mirrored in the confusion of terms in her speech: "Unfortunate lady that I am! I have left the herd on purpose to be chased, and have wandered this hour here; but the Park affords not so much as a satyr for me, and (that's strange) no Burgundy man or drunken scourer will reel my way" (V, ii). The resemblance of Lady Flippant to Fletcher's Cloe as she ranges the wood in search of any available prospect is in itself an allusion to pastoral ideal. But the nature of her moral imperfection is illuminated in the distortion of her speech. There is sufficient pastoral connotation in "herd," "park," "satyr" to remind us of the ideal standard upon which we are to judge the lady. Yet "herd" and "satyr" also reveal the bestiality of her nature, that sexual excess which causes her to misperceive the ideal. The further confusion of these terms on the one hand with Restoration slang ("Burgundy man," "scourer") and on the other with the elevated style of romance ("Unfortunate lady that I am") is a satiric commentary upon this middle-plane character and consequently upon the age. It suggests not only immorality but also the affectation of elegance as a mask for moral deformity. Style here, then, strikes a comparison between what love should be and what it has become and indicates the causes of the decay of virtue.

This same moral blindness and confusion of values is revealed in the passages wherein the speech of the morally deformed, middle-plane characters parodies the romantic discourse of the high characters. For example, the exchanges of Lady Flippant with Dapperwit, whom she pursues and who despises her, parody in manner and style the debates of Valentine and Vincent upon the nature of jealousy quoted above.

> LADY FLIPPANT: I hope you do not censure me because you find me passing away a night with this fool:—he is not a man to be jealous of, sure.
> DAPPERWIT: You are not a lady to be jealous of, sure.
> L.F.: No, certainly.—But why do you look as if you were jealous then?
> DAP: If I had met you in Whetstone's park, with a drunken foot-soldier, I should not have been jealous of you.
> L.F.: Fy, fy! now you are jealous, certainly; for people always, when they grow jealous, grow rude:—but I can pardon it since it proceeds from love, certainly.
>
> .   .   .   .
>
> Sweet Mr. Dapperwit, be not so censorious (I speak for

> your sake, not my own), for jealousy is a great torment,
> but my honour cannot suffer certainly.
>
> DAP: No, certainly; but the greatest torment I have
> is—your love.
>
> L.F.: Alas! sweet Mr. Dapperwit, indeed love is a tor-
> ment, but jealousy is a bitter torment—I do not go
> about to cure you of the torment of my love.   [I, ii]

Wycherley's satiric method here anticipates his method in
the "perfectly, perfectly" exchanges between Horner and
Lady Fidget in *The Country Wife*. His device is to play the
surface elegance of the character's diction against the base
corruption of his motives. Here, however, the satiric effect
serves an additional function in the pastoral design. Because
it parodies Valentine's romantic discourse, it renders distinct
the distance between the inferior natures of the middle characters and the perfection of the ideal characters. Flippant's
mimicry of romantic debate and her elevated style at once
prove her affected and stand as a commentary upon her
depravity. Dapperwit's repeated attempts to draw the level
of conversation from the high to the middle plane, while they
serve to deflate Flippant, and reveal his own vulgarity and
ignorance of the ideal, also sharply reveal the degree to
which they both deviate from the standard set by the high
characters.

Wycherley uses a second kind of parody which is intended
as a corrective of the more extravagant excesses of pastoral
style. An example is the conversation of Lydia with Dapperwit:

> LYDIA: Pray, sir, how are you dignified or distinguished
> amongst the rates of wits? And how many rates are
> there?
>
> DAPPERWIT: There are as many degrees of wits as of
> lawyers, . . . so there is first your court wit, your coffee

wit, your poll-wit . . . your chamber-wit or scribble-wit,
and last of all, your judge-wit, or critic. [II, i]

Dapperwit's hairsplitting differentiation and categorizing
mocks the manner of the romantic debate. However, while
the parody here is a satiric thrust at literary extravagance,
it is also a commentary upon Dapperwit and the whole
middle-plane outlook. Dapperwit is a would-be wit rather
than a true wit, because he thinks that to be a wit one need
only imitate the superficial verbal mannerisms of the true
wit. This corresponds exactly to the error of Flippant, who
thinks that to be a true woman of virtue one need only adopt
the romantic jargon of one's model. The middle-plane characters, and hence the Restoration audience itself, have fallen
from excellence because they have failed to recognize the
abstract principles that motivate excellence and have settled
for outward appearance alone. The consequence is that the
outward affectation of excellence is used by them to mask
inner deformity.

It must be granted the middle characters, however, that
they are able to perceive the ideal at least to the extent that
they can imitate its surface characteristics. The pure light
of the ideal barely penetrates the lowest level of the hierarchy. Just as he does in creating the high plot, in the low
plot Wycherley adapts without change the vision of his
model, Jonson. The groundwork for the satire of *The Plain
Dealer,* where vice is so obscene that it disgusts, is laid in
the creation of the low-level plane of this first play. It is
highly probable that the low plot characters were designed
with certain actors in mind, for each of the roles was played
by an actor famous for some interpretation of Jonson.
Mrs. Joyner was played by Mrs. Corey, referred to by theat-
rical chroniclers of the time as "Dol Common" because of
the excellence of her portrayal of that character in *The Al-
chemist.* Gripe was played by Lacey, famous for Sir Politic

Would-Be, Ananias, and Otter. Dapperwit was played by
Mohun, the "Face" and "Volpone" of the Restoration stage.[8]
Wycherley imitates not merely the tone and diction of his
master but his satiric technique as well. The exaggeration,
to grotesque effect, of the moral deformity of these characters
is achieved through a sharp concentration upon physical
processes. Love, the delightful abstraction of the Fletcherian
high plot, becomes in the low plot a gross, lip-smacking
physical act that "makes the belly swell." Human nature on
the low level is not merely distorted but completely deformed. The contest on the high level is between perfect
faith and jealousy, romantic abstractions. On the middle
level it is between male and female wit, contemporary actu-
alities. But on the low level it is between lechery and avarice,
universal deformities. Alderman Gripe's attachment to Lucy
is motivated by sexual appetite alone. The gross carnality of
his passion appears in the quality of his speech, for the language of love on the low level is expressed in images of
food consumption. "No, I am not dainty," Gripe asserts,
contemplating the prospect of possessing Lucy. "While you
talk of treats you starve my eyes; I long to see the fair one;
fetch her hither" (III, iii). Lucy is his meat, that which he
must buy to feed his raging lust. But in Gripe raging lust
contends with raging avarice; to satisfy both demons he
must buy Lucy at the lowest possible price. Lucy and her
mother, Mrs. Crossbite, prove his match in greed. When the
bawd, Mrs. Joyner, approaches them on his behalf, she meets
with some resistance, for they already have a source of income
in Dapperwit. The debates of Mrs. Crossbite and Mrs. Joyner
are a distance indeed from the love problems that concern
Valentine and Vincent.

> MRS. CROSSBITE: Mr. Dapperwit! Let me tell you, if
> 'twere not for Master Dapperwit, we might have lived

8. Cf. Noyes, *Ben Jonson,* passim.

all this vacation upon green cheese, tripe and ox cheek.
If he had it, we should not want it . . .

MRS. JOYNER: So, then, you are the dog to be fed, while
the house is broken up! I say, beware! The sweet bits
you swallow will make your daughter's belly swell,
mistress . . .   [III, i]

At this, the nadir of the pastoral hierarchy, human commerce
is reduced to commodity exchange. Yet even here the falling
off in human nature is measured by the degree to which it
deviates from the ideal. Again Wycherley employs the device
of planting in the low diction of these characters glaring
allusions to the standard upon which we are to measure them.

MRS. JOYNER: . . . His [Dapperwit's] bewitching mad-
rigals have charmed thee into some heathenish imp
with a hard name.

LUCY: Nymph, you mean, godmother.   [III, i]

As these characters are monstrous distortions of ideal human
nature, so is their speech a monstrous distortion of ideal expression. Their excesses are measured in the degree to which
their crude diction clashes with the allusions to romance
that stud it. The way in which they distort romantic diction
reflects exactly the way in which their vices distort human
nature, so that, for example, in their discourse all of the ideal
connotations of the word "nymph" vanish and we are left
with this perception of brutish ignorance: "A heathenish
imp with a hard name."

Yet even at this final reduction the human animal is not
simple. Wycherley, ignoring the contemporary critical bias,
follows Jonson directly, realizing that Cobb and Tib are the
same kinds of hypocrites as their betters. The comic effect is
broader when Lucy Crossbite employs elevated diction to
disguise her base motives than when Lady Flippant does.
But the device is exactly the same. It is merely that Lucy,

being less adept at hypocrisy, shows materialistic under-
pinnings:

> LUCY: Leave sweet Mr. Dapperwit!—Oh furious in-
> gratitude! Was he not the man that gave me my first
> Farrendon gown, put me out of worsted stockings and
> plain handkerchiefs, taught me to dress, talk, and move
> well?   [III, i]

Lucy's horror of ingratitude is the flimsiest of disguises for
her grasping greed. Her hope is that Dapperwit will bring
her into the playhouse, "where I might have had as good
luck as others . . . good clothes, plate, jewels . . ." When she
discovers that Gripe will provide well for her, she is quick
to transfer her allegiance.

We find the same confusion of values in the diction of
the low-level characters that we found on the middle plane,
but here incongruities are exaggerated to emphasize the
degree to which these characters are distorted. In their diction materialistic and idealistic imagery clash in jarring
confusion. Consider Dapperwit's lament at Lucy's plan to
break faith with him; "Can you have the heart to say you
will never more break a cheese-cake with me at New Spring
Garden . . ?" Satire here is two-edged; it slashes at human
affectation for pretending to the elegance of romance at the
same time as it slashes at vice-ridden human nature for falling below the ideal.

Still, the hypocrisy of Dapperwit and Lucy, wherein
lechery and greed crudely attempt to disguise their naked-
ness in rag-tag patches of romantic diction, is less offensive
than that of Alderman Gripe—the satyr of the pastoral
scene. Wycherley's satire is darkest in this characterization;
it anticipates the satire of his most finished work, *The Plain
Dealer*. In Gripe hypocrisy is not merely folly, the mask of

vice, but is itself vice. Gripe's diction is consequently not easily differentiated into mask and man. The words that express his hypocrisy cannot be separated from those that express his greed and his lechery. His diction is all of a piece and all expressive of his complete moral deformity. Significantly, his hypocritical diction does not affect imitation of romance diction, the ideal standard in the scheme of the play. It affects holiness rather than romance. His diction blends in inextricable mixture, false holiness, false humility, and greed, both sexual and mercenary. For example, he says, "There can be no entertainment to me more luscious and savory than communion with that little gentlewoman." "Communion" and "gentlewoman" express Gripe's Puritan cant as well as his false humility. He certainly does not mistake Lucy for a gentlewoman; he considers her a social inferior whose services his money enables him to buy. He marries her at the end only to protect his fortune from his new son-in-law, Dapperwit, avarice being stronger in him than any social consideration. "Luscious" and "savory," examples of the imagery of food consumption that riddles his speech, express the gross carnality of his desire, and "entertainment" his perception of the love relationship. Allowing that this last word had connotations in the seventeenth century different from those which it has today, I think that we can still say that in Gripe's materialistic perception commerce between the sexes is not part of the real business of life but a luxury, a purchased commodity, "entertainment." As even this small sample illustrates, hypocrisy does not appear as sugar coating in Gripe's discourse, but is an integral part of his expression. Gripe, the lowest figure in the hierarchy, the Sullen Shepherd of the piece, exhibits the incurable basic deformity of the satyr. He symbolizes human nature in its ugliest, most corrupt state.

In his first play, then, Wycherley exhibits the skill in

satiric technique that marks the finished quality of his mature plays. But in part because at this early stage his is a Renaissance sensibility, these appear as brilliant effects in a loosely structured Renaissance pastoral design. In *Love in a Wood* he draws the crucial comparison between the yearned-for ideal and the corrupt actuality, but his focus is upon St. George rather than the dragon. Here at the beginning he chooses the shepherd, not the satyr, as his spokesman.

Formally considered, Wycherley's second play, *The Gentleman Dancing Master,* is his only comedy. Borrowing his central plot device from Calderon's *El Maestro del Danzar,* he extends it into a structure that, though somewhat obvious and flimsy, answers the demands of the classical comic mythos: the outwitting by the clever innocent of senex, who would obstruct the progress of true love, and the final triumph of true love in an end-scene wedding that unites not just the lovers but all members of the human community whatever the nature or degree of their initial deviation from the ideal.

Perhaps because it so obviously fulfills our expectations of comedy, it has found favor with critics of this and the last century. Ward thought it "less exceptionable and more uniformly pleasing than *The Country Wife";* Summers prefers it to *Love in a Wood;* and, in our own day, Holland considers it worthy of a whole section of his book. The more discriminating Restoration courtly audience rejected it out of hand, though it found some favor when revived for the "cits," to whose chauvinism and complacency it might have appealed. Wycherley's account to Pope fixes the first composition of the play in 1661, but it was obviously hastily amended to take advantage of the patriotic fervor of the wartime audience of 1671, for most of its crude comedy rests upon the affirmation of everything English and the ridicule of everything foreign. Its satire, if it can be called that, is the superficial propaganda of a stand-up comedian entertaining the troops: for example, "to be a perfect Frenchman, you must never be silent, never sit still, and never be clean," or,

> MONS: [The Dutch] are only wise and valiant wen dey are drunkee.
> GER: That is, always. [I, ii]

For the most part, the satiric investigation of "humour," or universal human defect, degenerates in this atmosphere to the mere ridicule of exaggerated surface mannerisms of dress and speech.

The play, then, has little value as a work of art, but it can be useful in showing us the progress of Wycherley's development, and, more important, the constancy of his adherence to an ideal. Here, as in all his plays, the ideal is romantic love, with the accompanying virtues of honesty, modesty, courage. The defects of the imperfect characters are measured by their deviation from the ideal, and the causes of their deviation are materialism, which blinds them to the ideal, and hypocrisy. Just as Wycherley's ideal remains constant throughout his plays, varying only in the degree to which it seems attainable, so too does his central obsession with hypocrisy. The masks of false virtue, false modesty, false courage are the corrosives of human nature. Wycherley's subjects in the second play, then, are the same as those of the first; what differs is the focus of his vision. It is interesting to consider Wycherley's progress from pastoral to satire in terms of the Frye continuum.[9] Both pastoral and satire are unattainable extremes, the ends of the continuum that stretch toward perfect good and perfect evil, or, if you will, the opposite but equally intense visions of Heaven and Hell. Comedy and tragedy are visions within the human experience and of these tragedy is concerned with the heroically human. Only comedy draws in its boundaries to accommodate the

9. Frye, *Anatomy of Criticism.*

attainable, somewhat ridiculous vision of ordinary life. The end of tragedy is the preservation of an abstract metaphysical ideal; the end of comedy is a wedding and feast, the reaffirmation of the physical immortality of the human species through love.

The Gentleman Dancing Master is a middle step, a pause on the way from one extreme vision to its opposite extreme. Its form is the comic form; it scales down both the ideal and the anti-ideal, drawing them into the boundaries of the humanly attainable. The ideal here is the same in kind as the ideal of *Love in a Wood*—love and virtue—but it does not exist on the plane of airy abstraction. It is realized in realistic, Restoration terms. The anti-ideal is the same in kind as that in *Love in a Wood*—hypocrisy and materialism —but it does not exist on the plane of obscene Yahooism. It, too, is realized in Restoration terms as the folly of the fop, the prude, the jealous man.

The plot is simple. Don Diego, an Englishman turned Spaniard, with the caution of his adopted nationality has locked up his daughter to preserve her virtue and, consequently, his honor. He intends to marry her to her cousin, Monsieur de Paris, who affects Frenchness to the same ridiculous degree that his uncle affects Spanishness. Hippolita, the bride-elect, is determined not to marry her cousin but to find some means of getting a husband more to her liking. Playing upon Monsieur's vanity, she tricks him into sending Gerrard, the finest gentleman in the city, to her window. Gerrard and Hippolita are at once in love, but they are surprised in their first interview by Don Diego, who has just returned from Spain, and Mrs. Caution, Hippolita's prudish aunt and duenna. To save Hippolita's honor and her life, Gerrard goes along with her deception, that he is a dancing master sent by Monsieur de Paris to instruct her. The rest of the play revolves around the efforts of the lovers to come to an agreement while at the same time maintaining the

deception, and the subplot efforts of Don Diego to turn
Monsieur de Paris into a Spaniard.

Within this simple plot Wycherley makes the same differentiation that we found in *Love in a Wood,* between the
ideal and that which distorts, or deviates from, the ideal.
If the differentiation is not so obvious as it is in the first
play, that is because, answering the comic requirement,
Wycherley reduces the scope of this vision to ordinary life.
The world of this play is the contemporary Restoration
world. Consequently, action, diction, and tone here resemble
that of the middle plane of the first play. Here the difference
between ideal and less than ideal is revealed by means of
characterization. The heroine, Hippolita, though in action
and tone a Restoration tomrig, is nevertheless in character
a representative of ideal love. We come upon her and her
maid Prue lamenting in round Restoration style their con-
finement from the pleasures of the age.

> HIPP: To confine a woman just in her rambling age!
> take away her liberty at the very time she should use
> it! O barbarous aunt! O unnatural father! to shut up
> a poor girl at fourteen, and hinder her budding! . . .
> PRUE: 'Tis true, miss, two poor young creatures as we
> are!
> HIPP: Not suffered to see a play in a twelve-month!
> PRUE: Nor go to Punchinello, nor Paradise!
> HIPP: Nor to take a ramble to the Park nor Mulberry
> garden!
> PRUE: Nor to Totnam-Court, nor Islington!—
> HIPP: Nor to eat a syllabub in New Spring Garden
> with a cousin!
> PRUE: Nor drink a pint of wine with a friend at the
> Prince in the Sun!—

Except for an occasional snippet of high diction, Hippolita
speaks the language of her audience. She has all the stylistic

mannerisms of the contemporary sophisticated lady which, with her allusion to fashionable pastimes, mark her as a character with whom the audience can identify. Yet despite the realism of her diction, Hippolita is a romance heroine. The fashionable sophistication of her speech masks an innocence which, though militant in its own cause, is romantic. Wycherley's method is to set characters off against one another. In these opening lines, though both Prue and Hippolita assume a sophisticated tone, the difference of their motives is apparent. Prue's allusions reflect not just her social inferiority but the crudity of her desire as well. Hippolita may play at sophistication, but her natural modesty calls a halt when it is in the least threatened.

> HIPP: [Not suffered] to see a man!—
> PRUE: Nor come near a man!—
> HIPP: Nor hear of a man!—
> PRUE: No miss; but to be denied a man! and to have no use at all of a man!—
> HIPP: Hold, hold!—your resentment is as much greater than mine as your experience has been greater.   [I, i]

Hippolita is naturally virtuous—ideal love is here viewed as the natural condition, deviations from the ideal as distortions of nature. But her virtue is not passive. Her aim is to secure for herself a love relationship that is not tarnished by the base considerations that motivate those who surround her. Though she would enjoy the pleasures of the town, the pleasures she would enjoy are innocent, and her father who keeps her from those pleasures does so from a false sense of honor. Though she would employ the scheming wiles of her age to get herself a proper husband, the marriage she longs for is a love match, and her father and aunt who keep her confined do so from false senses of virtue. Though she would dangle her fortune before her lover's eyes to awaken his interest, she will not marry him, though she loves him, until he proves himself as idealistic as she by offering to take her penniless and in this action proves himself superior to her cousin, who acts from a false sense of manliness. Both Hippolita and Gerrard, the ideal woman and man, are distinguished from the other characters not only by their idealism but by their honesty and simplicity. Hippolita is the predecessor of Alithea in *The Country Wife,* the romantic heroine whose virtue and modesty being true qualities have no need of surface affectation or display, and whose modernity indicates that old-fashioned virtues are still possible though the age is corrupt. Gerrard is the predecessor of the projected ideal of *The Plain Dealer.* He is a robust and honest Englishman. He cannot sing any but old English songs. His speech is plain English, unornamented by foreign locutions. Both of them, in their plain-dealing and the old-fashioned simplicity of their virtues, anticipate the lost ideal for which the satires yearn. Yet in this play the ideal is still attainable. From the first quite realistic encounter of the lovers romantic love and modesty triumph over sophistication.

> HIPP: I h-h- like this man strangely, I was going to say loved him. Courage then, Hippolita! make use of the only opportunity thou canst have to enfranchise thyself. Women formerly (they say) never knew how to make use of their time till it was past; but let it not be said so of a young woman of this age—my damned aunt will be stirring presently—well, then, courage, I say Hippolita. Thou art full fourteen years old—shift for thyself. [aside]
> GER: So! I have looked upon her so long, til I am grown bashful too. Love and modesty come together like money and covetousness, and the more we have the less we can show it. I dare not look her in the face now, nor speak a word. [aside]   [II, ii]

The modern boldness of their actions—the heroine's tricking a man to her window, the hero's breaking in and planning to steal the lady away—is carefully (if perhaps inartistically) undercut by their modesty and obvious virtue. The result is that the hero and heroine come off as perfect romantic lovers forced to strange expedients by a corrupt age.

Hippolita's ideal love is contrasted by turns with the sexuality of Prue, the prudishness of Mrs. Caution and the avarice of her father. Prue's is the voice of the libertine age which Hippolita's romantic idealism, presented here as natural common sense, rejects.

> HIPP: Wouldst thou have me marry a fool, an idiot?
> PRUE: Lord! tis a sign you have been kept up indeed, and know little of the world, to refuse a man for a husband only because he's a fool! Methinks he's a pretty apish kind of a gentleman, like other gentlemen, and handsome enough to lie with in the dark, when husbands take their privileges; and for the day-times, you may take the privilege of a wife.
> HIPP: Excellent governess! You do understand the world, I see.
> PRUE: Then you should be guided by me.
> HIPP: Art thou in earnest then, damned jade?— wouldst thou have me marry him? Well, there are more poor young women undone, and married to filthy fellows by the treachery and evil counsel of chamber maids than by the obstinacy and covetousness of parents.
>
> [I, i]

Prue's perception, distorted by a base appetite too long denied, makes no discrimination between men. To her, love, as her opening lines reveal, is to "have use of a man." At her level of vision, which corresponds to that of the low plane characters in *Love in a Wood,* human commerce is the exchange of material satisfaction. Any man will do for her, for all serve equally well as instruments of satisfaction. They are mere objects to her, as she reveals when she talks of "taking up with her mistress's leavings," the "frenchified fool," Monsieur. Prue is too far below the ideal to consider its motivations or methods anything more than foolish nicety.

Yet Prue's appetite, however base, is merely a deviation from the ideal. It does not distort the natural as the greed or hypocrisy of the other imperfect characters do. Don Diego, for example, would marry his daughter to a fool to protect his fortune. Measured against the ideal, his conception of marriage is clearly only socially sanctioned prostitution. As Hippolita observes:

> The match soon made is happy still,
>   For only love has there to do.
> Let no one marry 'gainst her will,
>   But stand off when her parents woo,
> And only to their suits be coy:
>   For she whom jointure can obtain,
> To let a fop her bed enjoy,
>   Is but a lawful wench for gain.   [II, ii]

Don Diego, as well as the other imperfect characters, deviates from the ideal because his materialism will not allow him to see the abstract concept of honor that motivates the ideal. But beyond his deviation from perfection is the graver error of hypocrisy. Exactly reversing the pattern of Gerrard and Hippolita, who cloak their natural virtue in the sophistication demanded by the age, the hypocrites disguise their base natures by assuming a surface pose of honor. Wycherley strips Don Diego of his Spanish honor by showing its resemblance to the pose of the ladies of honor, the prostitutes Flirt and Flounce. Act I ends with the capture by Flirt and Flounce (who have been protesting their "honor") of Mon-

sieur de Paris. As he is being dragged off to the bordello,
Monsieur begs that they will have a care of his honor:

> MONS: But you will promise then to have the care of
> my honour? pray, good madam, have de care of my hon-
> our. Will you have de care of my honour? pray have de
> care of my honour, and do not tell if you can help it;
> pray dear madam, do not tell.   [I, ii]

Monsieur's honor is the good opinion of the world; nothing
is sin that is secret. Juxtaposed against this are the opening
lines of Act II, wherein Don Diego investigates the condition
of his honor:

> DON: [to Mrs. Caution] Have you had a Spanish care
> of the honour of my family? That is to say have you
> kept my daughter close in my absence as I directed?
>   [II, i]

The comparison makes two points. First, it reveals the falsity
of Don Diego's Spanish honor by comparing it with that of
Monsieur. And then it compares Don Diego with Flirt and
Flounce. The pseudo-Spaniard keeps his daughter locked up
because he will be able to get a good price for her if she is
virtuous. For him as for the "ladies of honor" love is legal
tender. The comparison is restated in the final scene. As
Monsieur with unwitting accuracy observes, there is no difference between marriage and keeping these days. Flirt's
attitude as she draws up the articles of provision for her keep
is compared with Don Diego's attitude toward marriage,
and both of these are sharply contrasted with the ideal
wedding of the lovers.

It is not just the avarice of the imperfect characters that
reveals their materialism. On the simplest level of farce
Don Diego thinks that Spanish pride is achieved with the
donning of a golilla and long hose. Monsieur de Paris, the
forebear of a long line of Restoration fops—(an honor

usually accorded Etherege's Sir Fopling Flutter[10]) is guilty of the error of all of them. He thinks that to be a man of mode one need only dress the part, with the added folly that the mode he imitates is French. He worships the pantaloons, ribbons, and ruffles that in his eyes make the man. In him Wycherley takes the Jonsonian humor character halfway to being the Restoration would-be wit. Both these fools scorn the plain English robustness of Gerrard—in the framework of this play the equivalent of unadorned natural manliness —because their attention is arrested at the surface level of physical ornament and cannot penetrate to such abstract qualities as virtue, courage, etc.

The implications of this error are more grave as they are presented in Mrs. Caution. Mrs. Caution's morality has been arrested at the surface level. Virtue for her is not an abstract ideal but a physical condition. She has not the ability granted Hippolita of distinguishing between good and evil, she can deal only with the material facts.

> HIPP: ... I never lived so wicked a life as I have done this twelve month, since I have not seen a man.
> MRS. CAUTION: How, how! If you have not seen a man how could you be wicked? How could you do any ill?
> HIPP: No, I have done no ill, but I have paid it with thinking.
> MRS. CAUTION: O that's no hurt! to think is no hurt:— the ancient, grave, and godly, cannot help thoughts.
>
> . . . .
>
> HIPP: But know I have had those thoughts sleeping and waking: for I have dreamt of a man.
> MRS. CAUTION: No matter, no matter so that it was but a dream: I have dreamt myself ...
> HIPP: But I did not only dream—

10. *The Man of Mode* first appeared in 1676, after all Wycherley's plays except *The Plain Dealer* had already been produced.

MRS. CAUTION: How, how! Did you more than dream?
speak young harlotry, confess . . .
HIPP: . . . Indeed, aunt, I did not only dream, but I was
pleased with my dream when I awaked.
MRS. CAUTION: Oh, is that all? . . .
HIPP: Ay, but to be delighted when we wake with a
naughty dream, is a sin, aunt . . . I would as soon consent to a naughty man as to a naughty dream.   [I, ii]

Hippolita is here, of course, playing the adversary for the
purpose of unmasking Mrs. Caution's disguised lust—a device which Wycherley will use to brilliant effect in the
satires. But in this scheme the exchange is used to contrast
natural virtue, which has no need of disguise, with the virtue
of the prude, which is merely lust in masquerade.

Wycherley's characteristic obsession with mask, which in
the mature plays is evidenced in such complex satiric prob-
ing of character, is, on the whole, rather simply manifested
in *The Gentleman Dancing Master*. Hypocrisy rarely penetrates below surface affectation. However, in one character,
the author does faintly indicate the direction that his concern with mask will take. The desires of Monsieur de Paris
and Mrs. Caution show through their masks, but Don Diego,
when his inner feeling does not match the image he has of
himself, adjusts his private feeling to suit his public personality. At the end of the play, for instance, when he finds
himself duped by the lovers but powerless to alter the situation, he pretends that he has not only been aware of the
deception all along but has himself contrived the situation,
having found his nephew a fool:

DON: [Aside] Robbed of my honour, my daughter,
and my revenge too! O my dear honour! Nothing vexes
me, but that the world should say I had not Spanish
policy enough to keep my daughter from being de-
bauched from me. But methinks my Spanish policy

might help me yet: I have it—so—I will cheat 'em all;
for I will declare I understood the whole plot and con-
trivance, and connived at it. . . . I am resolved to turn
the cheat upon themselves, and give them my consent
and estate.   [V, i]

Wycherley's awareness of the public self and the private self,
of the conflicts that arise between them, of the attempts by
the one image to dupe the other was to serve him in good
stead when he was obliged to grapple with the satyr-satirist
figure of the English satiric tradition, and to wring, from the
complex compound presented him, his own unique satiric
spokesmen, Horner and Manly.

Wycherley's early plays, then, were the proving ground
of techniques that he was to employ in his master works. The
loose pastoral plan of the first play and the prefabricated
comic pattern of the second freed him from structural problems and allowed him the liberty to develop satiric techniques before he was obliged to answer the severe demands
of the satiric structure. In addition it is fitting somehow that
the early plays prove the satirist's black vision to be only the
shepherd's vision distorted by its confrontation of corrupt
reality.

3. The Mature Plays

As long as men are false and women vain
While gold continues to be virtue's bane
In pointed satire Wycherley shall reign.

—Evelyn

Part I. Characterization of the Satiric Spokesman:
"The Satyr's Voice"

Satyre lashes Vice into Reformation, and humour represents folly so as to render it ridiculous. Many of our present Writers are eminent in both these kinds; and particularly the Author of the *Plain Dealer,* whom I am proud to call my Friend, has oblig'd all honest and vertuous Men, by one of the most bold, most general, and most Useful Satyres which has ever been presented on the English Theatre.[1]

This passage, besides giving evidence of Wycherley's status as a satirist in his own day, makes a useful critical differentiation. Dryden's key words, "satyre" and "humour," can be thought to represent the two related yet quite different streams that contribute to form Wycherley's conception of satire. "Satyre" might refer to the newly sharpened interest of Restoration critics, especially the foremost among them, Dryden himself, in the formal aspects of ancient satire. "Humour" might stand for the Restoration's satiric inheri-

1. Dryden, "The Author's Apology for Heroique Poetry and Poetique Licence" (preface to *The State of Innocence*), in *Dryden: The Dramatic Works,* ed. Montague Summers (London, 1932), 3, 419.

tance from the Renaissance. The former stream is thoroughly Roman, a product of the direct influence of classical critical theory upon Restoration aesthetics. The latter is as thoroughly English, grafting borrowings from ancient practice upon a basically English conception. In Wycherley's two attempts to render formal satire in the dramatic mode, *The Country Wife* and *The Plain Dealer*, these two satiric streams converge. The structure of his satires is based upon the new Restoration perception of the form of ancient satire; his characterization, particularly of the satiric spokesman, grows out of Renaissance theory and practice.

In *The Cankered Muse* Kernan confirms Campbell's theory[2] that the Elizabethans were more concerned with the intention of satire than with its form. Consequently, in their satiric composition the personality of the spokesman, the outraged scourge of Heaven, whose ministry is harsh reformation, is paramount. The traditional use of satire as an instrument of reformation combined with a false conception of the origin of ancient satire that derived it from the Greek satyr play was the kernel that informed all Elizabethan theories of satiric decorum, and that led in Elizabethan practice to the creation of the uniquely English satiric spokesman, whom Kernan calls the "satyr-satirist."

The evolution of this figure was a centuries-long process that began in the dim, preliterary English past and came to full flowering under the shaping influence of Renaissance humanism. There have been two schools of thought regarding the origin of English satire. One holds that the earliest English satire is goliardic—witty and gay. This joyful tradition is supposed to have held sway until the late fourteenth century, when religious reformers, following in the footsteps of St. Jerome and his idol, Juvenal, overwhelmed the good-

2. O. J. Campbell, *Comicall Satyre in Shakespeare's Troilus and Cressida* (San Marino, 1938).

natured native satire with their bitter *saeva indignatio*.[3]
The other school, taking a longer view, rests its theory upon
the supposition of a relationship between ancient English
and Celtic satire. It maintains that cruel and bitter satire is
the native growth[4] and finds its roots in the niðing verses
and bismeorleod of the Anglo-Saxon poet-magician. The
aim of the first English satirists, this theory asserts, was the
word-death of their enemies, a verbal murder practiced with
remarkable success in our own day by certain aborigines.
Like the modern witch doctor, the ancient English satirist
was able,

> to destroy his victim flesh and bone, nerve and sinew,
> his victim's hounds, cattle, pigs, wife and children . . .
> In other instances he meant to mutilate his victim's
> face so shamefully that . . . he could hold no high tribal
> office.[5]

The latter theory is the more credible for two reasons.
First, unsatisfied with twelfth- or thirteenth-century satire
as the first appearance of the genre, it traces satire
to an earlier period in the English tradition. Second, the
ferocity of the late medieval satirist, his use of word-surgery
in purging sin, his confidence in the awesome power of his
language, strike a marked resemblance to the traits of the
ancient poet-magician. The similarity strengthens the association between ancient English and Elizabethan English
satire, making it hard to conceive of *saeva indignatio* as a

3. Cf. G. R. Owst, *Literature and the Pulpit in Medieval England* (Cambridge, 1933).
4. Cf. M. C. Randolph, "The Medical Conception in English Renaissance Satiric Theory: Its Possible Relationships and Implications,"
Studies in Philology, 38 (1941), 125–57. R. C. Elliott, *The Power of
Satire* (Princeton, 1960), a comprehensive treatment of the origins
of satire, further proves this position and strongly supports the line
of development I have traced in this chapter.
5. Randolph, p. 129.

foreign importation of the late fourteenth century that completely supplants a diametrically opposed, goliardic native tradition. If, then, we hold with the theory of an Anglo-Saxon origin for English satire, we find that from the earliest times the satirist is a cruel and powerful being whose death-dealing language can destroy his victim or, at the least, cast him out from society.

In the atmosphere of social and religious reform that stirred England in the fourteenth and fifteenth centuries, the cruel satirist found not only ample opportunity for the exercise of his art but a perfect justification for his motives. His purpose, he declared, was sanative—his bitterness, despair at the sinfulness of men, his cruelty, a necessary scalpel to cut away the diseased member, his hatred reserved for the wilfully unjust. By the late fourteenth century, whatever was witty, gay, and probably Norman in origin disappeared from English satire.

> If the [late fourteenth century] satirist ever laughs at all, it is with a fierce and mocking laughter that bursts out suddenly without warning here and there, filled often with the spirit of mad exasperation and reckless despair.[6]

The dark bitterness of the English satirist's personality was becoming ever more firmly established in the tradition.

However, literature being more subtle in its view of human character than life, another dimension began to appear in the figure of the satirist-reformer as the poet perceived him. Literature, penetrating beyond his righteous surface, began to suspect his motives. The consequence is that his satiric outburst became two-edged, exposing not only his victims but sometimes himself as well. There entered into his fierce personality the suggestion of hypocrisy, and,

6. Owst, p. 216.

what is more, of hypocrisy masking sadism and corruption.
Chaucer's conception of the pulpit satirist, the pardoner,
provides the prime example of the complexity of the satiric
spokesman when he is transformed into a literary character.
As satirist-reformer, the pardoner's declared ministry is
scourging the sinful, and the force and efficacy of his bitter
abuse cannot be denied. His oratory does indeed reform his
audience, but that it does so is a side effect, an accidental
good, as

> ... many a predicioun
> Cometh ofte of yvel entencioun.

His real ends are selfish—"to ben avaunced by ypocrisye,"
"for veyne glorie," and "for hate." In the last of these aims
his satire is indeed complex. Language serves him as a weapon *because* he is impotent to hate by other means:

> For whon I dar noon other weyes debate
> Thanne wol I stynge hym with my tonge
>   smerte
> In prechyng ...   [413, 14]

From Chaucer we learn that the rage of the fourteenth-cen-
tury satirist-reformer is misplaced aggression, that he is guilty
of the corruption he attacks, that he attacks from hatred of
his victims not of their sins, that his bitter language is the
weapon of impotence and, finally, that religious reform is
not his true object but merely his mask:

> Thus spitte I out my venym under hewe
> Of holynesse, to semen hooly and trewe.[7]

With such a tradition behind him, the Renaissance hu-
manist approached ancient Roman satire with a perceptual

---

7. References are to *The Complete Works of Chaucer,* ed. F. N. Robin-
son (Cambridge, Mass., 1933).

set. A false theory of the origin of satire justified his precon-
ception of what a satiric spokesman should be, and Renaissance methods of imitation led him to ignore ancient theory
and to borrow from ancient practice only what he needed
to satisfy the demands of his own satiric decorum.

In his preface to the works of Terence (used universally
in Elizabethan schools), Donatus traced the origin of satire
through the *vetus comoedia* to the Greek satyr play. This
error, reinforced by the further error of deriving the word
"satire" from the Greek *satyros* rather than the Latin *satura,*
led the theorists of the Renaissance to associate satire with
satyrs. They concluded that in its most primitive form satire
was an attack delivered upon the audience by actors disguised
at satyrs. This concept of the origin of satire predetermined
the Renaissance view of ancient satiric practice. Puttenham,
commenting upon ancient satire, views the satyr's disguise
as a mask behind which the satirist conceals his identity and
by means of which he fortifies his attack:

> the first and most bitter invective against vice and
> vicious men was the Satyre; whiche to th' intent their
> bitterness should breed none ill-will . . . and besides
> making their admonitions and reproofs seeme graver
> and more efficacie, they made wise as if the gods of
> the woodes, whom they called Satyrs or Silvanes should
> appeare and recite those verses of rebuke.[8]

The aim of ancient Roman satire, consequently, was thought
to be harsh reformation—an aim consonant with the aim
of traditional native satire. The spokesman of ancient Roman
satire was thought to be the disordered, wildly raging beast-
man, the satyr—again, a figure certainly not dissonant with
the native English figure, the satirist-reformer.

---

8. Puttenham, *The Arte of English Poesie,* in *Elizabethan Critical Essays,* ed. G. Smith (2 vols. Oxford, 1909), 2, 32.

Renaissance methods of imitation fostered the misconception. The Renaissance approached the ancients not for guidance in forming theories of composition but either for the weight of authority to bolster its own aesthetic views (the approach to ancient literary theory) or for actual material to use in enriching its native literatures (the approach to ancient practice). The Italian critics and their English followers urged a theory of imitation based upon the conception of ancient literature as a warehouse of effects. They urged poets to plunder the ancients and to carry off whatever tropes, figures, locutions were needed to accomplish their own poetic aims.[9] In approaching ancient satire they ignored its subtle architecture, partly because the nature of their theory of imitation arrested their attention at the most superficial level of the poems, but also because the Renaissance aesthetic philosophy, being Christian in origin, was concerned with the intention, not the formal quality, of a work of art: "In telling a story we need not trouble ourselves whether it has a beginning, middle and end, but only whether it is fitted to its true purpose . . ."[1] As the "true purpose" of satire was harsh reformation, attention to formal architecture was not merely unnecessary, but actually detrimental. Structural design might be intrusive in a mode conceived as a savage outburst of righteous anger. The Renaissance writer of satire, then, might borrow the tone or the turn of wit of an ancient satirist, but he would not concern himself with the rules of Roman satiric composition. It is for this reason that Juvenal rather than Horace was the favored source. Horace was admired for lyric, Juvenal for satire. What the Renaissance satirist borrowed from Juvenal was his voice, his *saeva indignatio*.

9. Cf. Vida. *Poetica*, in *The Poetical Treatises of Horace, Vida and Boileau*, ed. A. S. Cook (Boston, 1892), p. 113.
1. Castelvetro, *Poetica*, as quoted by J. E. Spingarn, *A History of Literary Criticism in the Renaissance* (New York, 1925), p. 46.

However, since the false theory of the satirist as satyr
supported their conception of the satiric spokesman, Renaissance practitioners grafted new traits suggested by the satyr
image onto the image already existing in the native tradition. First among these was the irregularity of the satyr's
nature, which reinforced the theory that irregularity and a
rough style were appropriate in the savage outburst of the
satirist-reformer. Among the Elizabethan rules of satiric
decorum "the most important postulate was that satire, having originated in the mouths of shaggy creatures of the
Greek forests, ought to maintain the roughness and harshness which characterized their legendary actions. Even occasional obscurity might be cherished as proof that the
coarseness of these pristine goat-songs had not been refined
away."[2]

But beyond mere savagery, the image of the satyr super-
imposed upon the existent image of the satirist-reformer
heightened complex dimensions of the native figure that had
until now been merely suggested. In the satyr's savagery is
new justification for cruelty. Marston defends the tone of
The Scourge of Villanie as "sharp-fanged poesie" proper to
"a satyr's lippes." The satirist's pleasure in scourging for the
sake of personal revenge that was hinted in Chaucer's pardoner is fully developed when the satyr's character is added.
As Lodge says, "those monsters [satyrs] were then as our
parasites are now adayes, such as with pleasure reprehend
abuses."[3] But the most interesting contribution of the satyr
to the satirist is the emphasis and, indeed, explanation that
it provides for his moral duplicity. We saw in Chaucer that
the satirist's moral outrage was a mere mask of his personal
spite. When the satirist openly takes up a disguise, he calls

2. Campbell, p. 29.
3. Thomas Lodge, *Defence of Poetry*, in *Elizabethan Critical Essays, 1*,
   80.

attention to the disparity between his inner and outer personalities:

> Though in shape I seem a man
> Yet a satyr wilde I am

In addition, the wantonness traditionally associated with the satyr becomes the explanation of his need for a mask. He is guilty, at least in imagination, of the very vices against which he rages. Moreover, that he is guilty is what makes him rage. At first, as in the lines above, the disguise is very openly assumed, but finally the characteristics of the mask are assimilated by the "personality" of the satiric spokesman. The satyr's wantonness coarsens his diction, makes his manner obscene, but, most important, makes hypocrisy his most salient feature.

> An Executioner am I
> Of Lust and Wanton Venery
> Thus are vices scourged by me
> Yet myself from vice not free
> Like to Sumners that cite others
> When themselves defile their Mothers.[4]

In his fullest development, then, the Renaissance satyr-satirist is, as he was from the Anglo-Saxon period, cruel, ferocious, savagely courageous. Yet his nature is irregular, for added to these qualities are wantonness, envy, and duplicity.

Wycherley's Renaissance forebears were, of course, dramatists—dramatists who attempted the task that he at last accomplished, to render satire in the dramatic mode. But the Elizabethan dramatist turned satirist was faced with a unique problem. He had to create a suitable dramatic struc-

---

4. "Vice's Executioner," *The Workes of George Wither* (London, 1620), p. 308.

ture to accommodate a genre the very essence of which was thought to be its irregularity, and he had to characterize in drama a figure whose traits were predetermined by a non-dramatic tradition. The spokesman of verse satire can assume the role of satyr easily, since he merely acts and is not acted upon. In the drama he must present a more complex personality if he is to be more than a mere Morality play symbol. Of the three Elizabethan satiric dramas that attempt to deal with this problem—Jonson's *Every Man Out of His Humour,* Shakespeare's *Troilus and Cressida,* and Marston's *The Malcontent*—each provides a different solution to the problem of accommodating the satyr-satirist to a dramatic form suitable for satire. Each of the solutions emphasizes or develops aspects of the figure that can be of use to one who would understand Wycherley's characterization of Manly and Horner.

Jonson's play is interesting as an experiment in finding a proper structure for dramatic satire (for a conflict arose between the Elizabethan dictum that satire must be irregular and Jonson's usual obedience to structural regularity), but it is more interesting still for the refinements it makes upon the characterization of the satiric spokesman. Jonson's perplexity about form is immediately apparent. In the Induction —which is in itself an almost perfect verse satire, with Asper as satirist and Mitis and Cordatus as adversarii—the poet demonstrates his awareness, however unconscious it may have been, of the structure of Roman satire. But in constructing the play itself he rejects classical form. He brings his dilemma forward as an aesthetic problem in the critical speculations of Mitis and Cordatus. When Mitis asks whether Asper has observed the Terentian rules in creating his play, Cordatus explains that these are "too nice observations"; the usual rules cannot apply here. Jonson, following Donatus, looks to the Old Comedy as a secondary source of ancient satire. And since the writers of Old Comedy had neither models nor rules but were forced to devise their own,

Jonson cites their example to justify the necessity he was under to strike out in search of a new form, one that would answer the requirements of his own, Elizabethan satiric decorum.

> I see not, then, but we should enjoy the same license or free power to heighten our invention as they did; and not be tied to those strict and regular forms which the niceness of a few—who are nothing but form—would thrust upon us.[5]

In the construction of the play proper Jonson relies neither upon the classical rules for comic composition, nor upon his own first-hand familiarity with Roman verse satire. Instead he constructs a loose, irregular structure—an obvious attempt to realize the Elizabethan vision of satire as a rough-hewn, pristine goat song—through which parade a variety of stock comic types: Fungoso, the fop; Sogliardo, the upstart; Shift, the miles gloriosus. Because the characters as well as the contrived ending are comic, the play fails as satire. Comic characters cannot exemplify that monstrous vice with which satire must concern itself, and the comic ending, in which obstacles are overcome and order restored, is antithetical to the satiric vision. Satire, because its function is to expose universal and timeless corruption, must be open-ended. It must expose human vice, and though it may offer, by demonstration or implication, an alternative virtue, it must leave the resolution of the conflict to the reader or audience. Generically satire is destructive—it exposes evil—but not constructive—it does not present the triumph of good. *Every Man Out* fails as satire because it fails to provide an architecture proper to the satiric vision. The play is structurally valuable only in demonstrating the Elizabethan confusion about the formal aspects of satire.

5. *Ben Jonson,* ed. C. H. Herford and P. Simpson (11 vols. Oxford, 1927), 3, 432. All references are to this edition.

For our purposes the most significant contribution the play makes is to the development of the satiric spokesman. Recognizing the complexity, the strange combination of sometimes contradictory traits, that the Elizabethan satyr-satirist embodied, Jonson divides the figure into three separate characters. Asper, the *vir bonus,* who is portrayed as the writer of [1] the play, is Jonson's idea of himself, or of any poet who proposes to write satire. In his satiric exchange with Mitis and Cordatus, Asper displays the characteristics of the satirist-reformer. He writes, he declares, out of an outraged sense of justice. His aim is to cure society by forcing it to recognize its sin-scarred face:

> Well, I will scourge those apes
> And to these courteous eyes oppose a mirrour,
> As large as is the stage, whereon we act,
> Where they shall see the times deformitie
> Anatomized in every nerve and sinnew.
>
> [Induction]

Macilente, the disguise or "persona" assumed by Asper [2] when he engages in the action of the play, is a grotesque caricature of the satirist-reformer. More accurately, the characterization of Macilente is an exploration in the true nature of the satirist-reformer, the exposure of that in him which he is at pains to conceal from the world. Macilente's motivation is not an outraged sense of justice, but, on the contrary, is love and envy of the very vices against which he rails. He scourges men not to cure them of their evil, but to spite them for their advantages. He envies the miser his wealth, the fop his appearance, and the uxorious husband his wife. Although it is true that his machinations at last purge the fools of their excesses, he does not design them to that end. He prevents the cuckolding of Deliro and effects the cure of his uxoriousness neither out of regard for Deliro nor out of hatred for the sin of adultery or the folly of doting, but rather because his unrealizable passion for Deliro's wife makes him hate and envy her lover and her husband.

> Blind Fortune still
> Bestows her gifts on such as cannot use them
> How long shall I live 'ere
> I be so happy to have a wife of this exceeding form?

The cruel fury of the satirist makes him unmask the parasite Buffone, but it also drives him to the mean pettiness of poisoning Puntavarlo's dog. That he himself is cured of envy is a mere concession to the comic happy ending. In Macilente Jonson fully develops an aspect of the satirist's personality that had been mentioned earlier, but that had never been fully explored. The freedom to scrutinize the character so closely was granted by the greater objectivity that the dramatic mode permits.

(3)   Jonson conducts the exposure of the exposer still further in the characterization of Buffone. Buffone is neither as cruel in method nor as twisted in motive as Macilente. He is the satirist portrayed in still another, lighter vein—as one who ridicules and is himself rendered ridiculous. Moreover, in him Jonson explores another dimension of the satirist, his parasitism. While Macilente's envy of vice drives him to scourge men, Buffone's recognition of folly drives him to make use of it. Buffone is not driven mad by the sight of human corruption. Quite the contrary, he revels in it as a source of gain. For example, he recognizes that Sogliardo, the would-be courtier, is an ass. But rather than hating him as an upstart, Buffone pretends to undertake his training as a gentleman. When Sogliardo is not within hearing, Buffone ridicules his folly, but ridicule though he may, he also lives upon it. Buffone is as ready to detect vice in others as Macilente is, but he seeks out the fool not to purge him but to exploit him. He encourages folly in others for his own amusement and for his own profit. Buffone, because he promotes folly, is more involved in the scene of social corruption presented us than is Macilente. Macilente's cruel envy makes him an outcast from the company of men; his detachment makes him a strong figure in the satiric scene. Buffone is part of the scene; while he is often used as spokesman for satire he is, nevertheless, clearly of the company that is being satirized.

The development of these two aspects of the satiric persona into two separate characters (the envious malcontent-satirist, who is guilty, in desire or in fact, of the vices he rails at in others; and the more comical, clever parasite-satirist, who both ridicules and exploits the vices he detects) was a major contribution to the satiric tradition. These two figures became stock figures; their constant appearance was, in the words of Campbell, "the convention most distinctive of the new genre [dramatic satire]."[6] But equally important was Jonson's differentiation of both these figures from Asper, the poet who writes satire. The distinction between the poet and the satiric persona is one that we have persistently failed to recognize. It is, as Maynard Mack so cogently argues,[7] vitally important to the understanding of the genre.

In *Troilus and Cressida* Shakespeare once again unites in a single character the two faces of the satirist that Jonson had differentiated in Macilente and Buffone. Thersites is both the envy-driven malcontent and the parasite. Those traits that were outlined in Macilente are brought to full perfection in him. He is cruel, envious, and vicious. He is outcast from the society of his fellows. The vileness of his language is barely adequate to express the full vileness of his mind. He sees corruption everywhere, and in his vision human nature is diminished and distorted. To him the glorious Trojan war is no more than the argument of a cuckold

6. Campbell, p. 29.
7. "The Muse of Satire," in *Studies in the Literature of The Augustan Age,* ed. R. C. Boys (Ann Arbor, 1950), pp. 219–31.

and whore. Yet rail against corruption though he may, he is nevertheless a part of it—as corrupt as the scene upon which he comments. His moral position is neatly outlined in the scene in which he spies upon Ulysses and Troilus, while they are spying upon Cressida, who is arranging a tryst with Diomed. Thersites, at the furthest periphery from the center of evil, is nevertheless very much involved in it. He rails at the lust of the unfaithful Cressida and her new lover. Moving outward, he rails also at the lust of Troilus, which enslaves him to Cressida. On the furthest circle he stands, as filled with lust as his targets and envious of their power to find satisfaction. In the same way he rages against the combined strength and stupidity of the oxlike Ajax, at the same time that he envies the strength and admits that he would gladly exchange his cleverness for Ajax's stupidity, if stupidity brought with it strength and power. He would prefer that Ajax were the railer and he the beater. In establishing motivation for Thersites' raging satire, Shakespeare develops an idea that we found in germ in Chaucer's pardoner and saw developed in Jonson's Macilente, the idea that railing is in itself pleasurable to the satyr-satirist and is his means of compensating for some deficiency. Being by some means —cowardice, ugliness, sexual inadequacy—barred from the activities of normal men, he uses hostile and obscene language as the release of his envy and frustration and as a substitute for action. The language of satire, which had been a real weapon for the ancient English poet-magician and the medieval reformer, has in the mouth of the Elizabethan satyr-satirist dwindled into a toy, a mock weapon that does no injury to its target and grants no power to its speaker. It effects no cure, nor is it meant to. Rather, it calls to our attention the corruption of the scene before us; and while it exposes the vices of other characters, it also exposes the envy of vice, the hypocrisy and the impotence of the speaker.

To these traits, which are a fuller development of Macilente's character, Shakespeare adds the parasitism of Jonson's Buffone. But the parasitism is first stripped of its comic associations. Thersites' parasitism has nothing of the lightness of a Jonsonian parasite. Buffone ridicules his hosts, but he has for them that contemptuous affection that the con-man has for his pigeon. Thersites, on the other hand, bitterly hates those upon whom he lives, Ajax and Achilles. In this, however, Shakespeare runs counter to Renaissance convention, which associates the malcontent satirist with dark, bitter satire and the parasite satirist with a lighter, more comical satire.

The characterization of Thersites contributes three ideas to the developing satyr-satirist. First, Thersites is not foolish but monstrous in his vice. Second, he is at once a commentator upon and a participant in the scene of vice presented us. Finally, his language underscores the corruption of the scene before us, but it effects no cures, promotes no happy endings. It is rather a double-edged weapon that unmasks the speaker and his victims at the same time.

Marston's *The Malcontent,* though a conventional melodrama rather than an attempt to render satire dramatically, nevertheless makes an interesting addition to the satyr-satirist's progress. In this play the traits of the satyr-satirist are used as a mask, to implement action which is not satiric. We are led, from the descriptions that precede his entrance, to expect in the hero the conventional malcontent satirist. He is described as

> a man, or rather, a monster; more discontent than Lucifer when he was thrust out of the presence, his appetite as insatiable as the grave, as far from any content as from Heaven; his highest delight is to procure other's vexation and therein he thinks he truly serves Heaven; for 'tis his position whoever in this earth can be contented is a slave and damned; there-

> fore do's he afflict all in that which they are more
> affected; the Elements struggle within him . . . his
> speech is halter-worthy at all howers . . .[8]   [I, ii]

The discontent, the cruelty, the irregularity of nature, the
obscenity of speech, all the traits most characteristic of the
satyr-satirist, are attributed to Malevole. His name itself
distinguishes him. At first he seems quite to fulfill our expectations. He thrusts at his victims (the wanton wives, upstarts,
obsequious hypocrites—the stock types of satire) with vigor.
A typical greeting is:

> And how do's my olde Muckhill o'erspread with fresh
> snow, thou halfe a man, halfe a goat, all a beast, how
> do's thy young wife, olde huddle?

As the plot unfolds, however, we learn that this manner,
like his name, is assumed. He is not Malevole, the satyr-
satirist, but the good Duke of comedy who has, as one might
expect, been deposed and whose business is to effect the
romantic resolution that will restore order. The stock comic
types—the Machiavel, the evil woman and the chaste, romantic one—support this action.

The interesting contribution of this play to the line we
have been following is to prove that by the time Marston
writes, the traits of the satyr-satirist are so familiar that they
have hardened into a mask. They can be relied upon to elicit
a particular response. But the use to which this mask is put
itself contributes to the complexity of the characterization.
The hero assumes the mask of satyr-satirist to divert attention from his real aims which are not satiric but comic. The
complexity is almost endless. The mask of the satyr was
assumed by the satirist; the mask of the satyr-satirist was
assumed by the malcontent; now these in combination have

8. *The Plays of John Marston*, ed. H. Harvey Wood (3 vols. Edinburgh,
1934), *1*, 146. All references are to this edition.

hardened into a mask which is assumed by one whose aims are not satire at all. Marston adds yet another dimension to the Elizabethan vision of the character.

This fully developed figure, the product of centuries of grafting and emendation upon a basically English type, was Wycherley's inheritance. Only the predisposition of critics to cut off Restoration drama from the rest of the literary tradition could have blinded them to this line of development. Isolating the period has led them to more serious errors. Because Manly will not fit the image of that monster child of bad criticism "the Restoration comic hero," critics have been led into the fallacy of confusing the poet with his creation—they have assumed that Manly is a self-portrait. Moreover, adding the insult of thinking the poet witless to the injury of thinking him obvious, they accuse Wycherley of their own error, of confusing himself with a character in the play of still another poet.

> Alceste out of touch with the society in which he moved, how much he was Wycherley himself! Alceste who craved honesty above all things, was this not also Wycherley with his reputation for outspokenness . . . Wycherley threw himself into the character, and with his rage for the absolute came to an extreme of furious passion, imagining himself in the worst conceivable situations, so that every event would prove him right in his indignation.[9]

It has even been suggested that the characterization of Manly confirms "our suspicions that [Wycherley] was not 'born' a Restoration gentleman."[1] Oddly enough, these same critics accept Horner as a perfect Restoration hero. They are scarcely troubled by the question why Wycherley should have been in accord with his age in 1674, when *The Country*

9. Bonamy Dobrée, *Restoration Comedy* (London, 1924), p. 87.
1. Lynch, *The Social Mode of Restoration Comedy*, p. 174.

Wife appeared, and so violently at odds with it in 1675, when *The Plain Dealer* was first presented. The answer to this question varies with the critic, but generally the consensus is that Wycherley suffered a kind of artistic schizophrenia, that *The Country Wife* expresses that in him which loved to revel in the wicked age while *The Plain Dealer* expresses the triumph over that baser self of Wycherley's "puritan instincts" (cf. Dobrée, Lynch, and others). This is wholly fallacious reasoning, springing from a basic theoretical confusion. Nothing in Wycherley's biography suggests that he "was out of touch with the society in which he moved." Quite the contrary, from the time that *Love in a Wood,* his first play, appeared and he was dubbed "son of a whore" (i.e. a wit) by the Duchess of Cleveland, Wycherley was in the very swim of courtly society. A favorite of his king and the ladies of the court, a wit, a beau, a keeper of mistresses, Wycherley the man was every inch a Restoration gentleman. The Restoration age was probably no more wicked than any other, but one thing is certain: it was much more intellectually and aesthetically aware than most.

However, Wycherley the man is of no consequence; it is Wycherley the poet who concerns us. If we would avoid the false reasoning of the critics, we must eliminate their fundamental error—the same that caused generations of critics to think of Pope as "the wicked wasp of Twickenham." To this end Maynard Mack has created the "muse of satire." In studying formal satire, he cautions

> We overlook what is most essential if we overlook the distinction between the historical Alexander Pope and the dramatic Alexander Pope who speaks them [the satires]. It is to underscore this distinction that I have ventured in my title to name the Muse. For the Muse ought always to be our reminder that it is not the author as man who casts these shadows on our printed

page, but the author as poet. . . . Moreover, the Muse ought to remind us that in any given instance the shadow might not delineate even the whole poet, but perhaps that angle of his sensibility which best refracts the light from epic, elegy, pastoral, lyric, satire.[2]

In choosing to write satire Wycherley took upon himself responsibility for a well-established genre. We assume that he called into play that angle of his sensibility that best refracted the light from satire, but his personal motives for writing are irrelevant. It is obvious that Wycherley was keenly aware of the demands of both of the satiric traditions that unite in him. The characterization of the satiric spokesman, Manly and Horner, must be understood in the light of the long English tradition outlined above. Manly, because he is part of a dark satiric design, follows the line set for him by the bitter malcontent satirist of Elizabethan convention. Horner, because he is part of a lighter satiric design, follows the clever parasite–satirist of Elizabethan convention. Both of them clearly reflect the tradition that shaped them.

Manly fits to the last detail the Elizabethan model. As we have seen, the features that distinguish the satyr-satirist are "the virtues and failings of the uncivilized man."[3] Supposedly a descendant of Greek beast-men, this figure possessed those qualities traditionally associated with satyrs— on the one hand, reckless courage, strength, and hardihood; on the other, primitivism that gives rise to ungovernable passions, particularly rage and lust. All these are qualities that either supplement or reinforce the traits associated with the satirist-reformer of the middle ages—ferocity, harshness bordering upon sadism, and confidence in the awesome powers of his satiric language.

If Manly's name were not sufficient suggestion that he is

2. Mack, p. 222.
3. Kernan, p. 92.

the "natural man," his occupation and position relative to
the society in which he moves would mark him. Ordinarily,
the protagonists of the comedy of the period are men of
mode whose business is pleasure. Most of the characters of
The Plain Dealer are of the leisure class, and it is certainly
this class of society to whom the satire is addressed. It is singular, therefore, that Manly should be a sailor, and that his
occupation should be insisted upon again and again throughout the play, though it serves no function in the action. Traditionally, the figures in pastoral are bound either to the land
or the sea. Usually, as their name implies, they are shepherds,
but sometimes they are fishermen. What is essential to their
function is that they be bound to nature, uncultivated, ignorant of the ways of corrupt, hypocritical society. The
pastoral figures in Restoration drama retain this association,
though their worth relative to the society with which they
are contrasted varies with the playwright who employs them.
Most often they are country types, the Margerys and Prues,
the awkward Tony Lumpkins and drunken country lords
that we find represented in almost all these comedies. But
as often they are sailors. Ben in *Love for Love,* so awkward
in society that even Prue the country girl rejects him, is a
"great sea calf." Sir Wilfull Witwoud is a country bumpkin
on his way, when we meet him, to becoming a sea bumpkin.
In the Restoration scene the sailor and the country clout are
intruders from another world of experience. They are out-
casts from polite society, bunglers who understand neither
proper rules of conduct nor discreet methods of deception.
In all cases they are used to set off certain features of polite
society.

The sailor figure in Restoration drama, then, implies, first,
detachment from society, and, second, a "natural," uncivilized by polite standards. Manly, by occupation a primitive,
not only is a misfit in society, but his most fervent desire is
to escape it. His inclination is to "settle himself some where

in the Indies," a locale particularly associated in the minds
of the Renaissance and Restoration with the savage or primitive.[4] Manly is a savage by all counts. Even his men, themselves primitives, think him uncivilized. Their descriptions
that precede his entrance lead us to expect the satyr-satirist,
for we learn that he is recklessly brave, that he delights in
cruel combat, and that his courage is born of an unreasonable, ungovernable rage.

> 2ND SAILOR: . . . he's always as dogged as an old tar-
> paulin, when hindered of a voyage by a young panta-
> loon captain.
> 1ST SAILOR: 'Tis true I never saw him pleased but in
> a fight; and then he looked like one of us coming from
> the pay-table, with a new lining to our hats . . .
> 2ND SAILOR: A pox! He's like the Bay of Biscay, rough
> and angry let the wind blow where 'twill.
> 1ST SAILOR: Nay! There's no more dealing with him
> than with the land in a storm . . .   [I, i]

The awkward diction and seaman's locutions of the sailors
mark the degree of their deviation from polite society. Their
further distancing of Manly sets him altogether outside the
bounds of the society with which he will in the course of
the play engage. Manly is an outcast "bully tar," a savage
motivated by cruel rage. That rage can be manifested as
virtue—in prodigious fighting ability and boundless courage.
In his role of satirist–reformer it makes him a fearless scourge
of hypocrisy who does not hesitate to pull a hypocrite's nose
because he is an alderman or throw a flatterer down the
stairs because he is a lord. But that same rage can be manifested as unreasonable hatred. His anger falls impartially
upon the innocent as well as the guilty. Manly may box the

4. Cf. Frank Kermode, introduction to *The Tempest* (New Arden Edition, London, 1954).

ears of a lawyer whom he recognizes as a knave, but he accords the same treatment to a sailor for saving his life, damning him as "a fawning water spaniel" for his pains. If he scorns Freeman as a flattering opportunist, he scorns equally the innocent and loyal Fidelia. Manly's is the anger of Macilente or Thersites. Rage blinds him to the difference between good and evil and causes him to strike out wildly against the whole world.

As Kernan reminds us, in the Elizabethan mind "there was a vague but tenacious link between the writing of satire and an abnormal mental state variously identified as saturnine, malcontent . . . and finally melancholic."[5] The association was strengthened when the satirist became a figure in drama, for his personality accorded so well with that of the "melancholic" humour character. Manly, at core a Jonsonian humour character, is a malcontent. His hatred of hypocrisy and the excess to which he carries his harsh plain-dealing grow out of an irrational discontent that makes him reinforce his outcast state by viewing himself as one against the world. He sets his men with drawn cutlasses to guard his doors against the entry of hypocrites—that is, he explains, against everyone, since all the world are hypocrites and, consequently, all his enemies. His discontent is proud. He hates the greatest part of mankind, he observes, "only because they deserve it." He sets himself above, as well as outside, the company of his fellows, and like Shakespeare's Jaques he nourishes his discontent and prides himself upon it as a virtue. He refuses to recognize that this pride is merely self-love, an obsession with himself that makes him ignore the virtue that stands beside him in the loyal Fidelia to pursue a will-o-the-wisp reflection of himself in Olivia. Olivia reveals that she has used Manly's discontent and self-love to play upon him—"I knew he loved his singular moroseness

5. Kernan, p. 113.

so well as to dote upon any copy of it, whereof I feigned
hatred of the world too, that he might love me in earnest."

Like the Elizabethan satyr-satirist, Manly is, above all,
harsh and frank. The rage that before the action of the play
was released in warfare within the play becomes a whip to
scourge hypocrites. At his first entrance he comes hurtling
onto the stage soundly berating a lord.

> Tell not me, my good Lord Plausible, of your decorums,
> supercilious forms and slavish ceremonies! Your little
> tricks which you, the spaniels of the world, do daily
> over and over, for and to one another not out of love
> or duty, but your servile fear.   [I, i]

Throughout the play he braves hypocrisy and forces the
mirror of truth before its eyes. But often his speech, like
that of his forebears, degenerates into pointless railing. It is
"halter-worthy at all howers" casting damnation upon the
head of somebody in every line. There is some suggestion
that he hates his seamen less than the rest of the world, yet
he addresses them always as "dogs," "rascals," "spaniels,"
or "sea pimps." The bare forms of polite discourse are enough
to send him into a frenzy of railing against hypocrisy. Consequently, it becomes apparent that though his language is
often a real weapon against hypocrites, it is more often a release, a substitute for action. Chaucer's pardoner is by nature
impotent; Macilente and Thersites are rendered impotent by
cowardice; Manly's impotence is socially determined. When
he comes into society, his normal outlet for rage, namely
warfare, is denied him. Beyond the rather trivial ear-boxing
and nose-pulling, he is powerless to act. His hands are further tied by the fact that his most dangerous enemy is a
woman and better protected than men by the rules of civilized conduct. Having no outlet in action then, his rage wastes
itself in harsh satire. In Act II we are made sharply aware of
the function language serves for him. The returning warrior,

he seeks out his mistress only to learn that she has betrayed him. When she openly scorns him, he is filled with rage, but his normal response, which would be to strike her, is denied him, since he is in civilized society. He therefore seeks relief in speech, but even in this he is thwarted because he cannot think of language powerful enough to wound her. In his fury he alludes to the relation between the satirist's language and his impotence: "If I could say anything injurious to her now, I would, for I could outrail a bilked whore, or a kicked coward."

However, this failure of language as an effective substitute for action is momentary. A moment later we are given a glimpse of the power of the satirist's language, and his recognition of that power. Act II ends with a curious exchange that seems to be unmistakable evidence of Wycherley's awareness of the tradition in which he was working. Manly, the satirist, and Olivia, a kind of lesser satirist, engage in the most ancient and most English form of satiric exchange, a cursing. Olivia has been mocking Manly and is about to leave him and join the company at ombre.

> MANLY: . . . I'll wish you a little luck before you go.
> OLIVIA: . . . No, if you would have me thrive, curse me: for that you'll do heartily, I suppose.
> MANLY: Then, if you would have it so, may all the curses light upon you, women fear and you deserve! First, may the curse of loving play attend your sordid covetousness, and Fortune cheat you by trusting to her, as you have cheated me. The curse of pride or a good reputation fall on your lust; the curse of affectation on your beauty, the curse of your husband's company on your pleasures, and the curse of your gallant's disappointments in his absence; and the curse of scorn, jealousy, or despair on your love; and then the curse of loving on!

OLIVIA: And to requite all your curses, I will only return your last; may the curse of loving me still fall on your proud, hard heart . . . But heaven forgive you.
MANLY: Hell and the devil reward thee!   [II, i]

In the suggestion of primitive magic that pervades this passage we glimpse the ancient, awesome core of English satire. In her declaration that she thrives on curses Olivia alludes to that familiar property of witches. Manly is tempted to curse, and the seriousness of his cursing is revealed in his evocation of the forces of Hell. The efficacy of the curses is revealed in later action: Olivia *is* cursed with the pride of a good reputation on her lust; her husband's company indeed intrudes upon her pleasures; her gallant, the disguised Fidelia, must perforce disappoint her and must elicit her despair and jealousy. Manly, of course, is cursed precisely in "loving on." It is clear that the contestants recognize the terrible power of the satirist's language. Manly hesitates to release his linguistic power until Olivia goads him into cursing—"If you would have it so, then . . ." But when once his power is released, the comprehensiveness of his curse recalls the ancient poet-magician who casts a blight upon everything that might give joy to his victim. The full impression of the passage is of a weaker satirist-magician, Olivia, challenging the stronger, Manly, to a verbal battle that will determine whose is the more powerful magic.

We find in Manly's character, then, those traits that form the Renaissance conception of the satirist. He is a savage whose rage manifests itself at once as courage and as unreasonable cruelty. He is harsh and brutally frank. Moreover he shows the satirist's peculiar employment of language; it serves him both as a public scourge of social ill and as a personal outlet for violence that he cannot dissipate in action. Further, in a more primitive usage, it serves him as a personal weapon with which to injure his enemy magically. But there is another dimension of vice in the Elizabethan satyr-satirist that we have not yet sought in Manly: lust and the participation in the very vice which he attacks in others. The new Restoration adherence to Roman principles of composition in satire forbade the treatment of more than one principal vice. Other vices could be treated only as they arose from or were related to that under consideration. Hypocrisy being the central vice in *The Plain Dealer,* Wycherley could not employ the simple technique of having the satiric spokesman rail against lust and then showing him to be lustful, having him rail against avarice and then showing him to be avaricious, etc. He solves the problem by making the deterioration of Manly's character contingent upon his falling prey to the vice he most detests in others, namely hypocrisy. Manly becomes a hypocrite to hide the vices most closely associated with the Elizabethan satyr: lust and envy. As his character further degenerates, even those traits that we found admirable, if excessive, at the beginning of the play—raging courage and fearless honesty—are distorted into brutish sadism.

Manly's fall progresses slowly from his first venture in hypocrisy to the full triumph of his worser self. His first hypocritical gesture is the result of trying to hide from Freeman (whose scorn he fears) the fact of his unquenchable desire for Olivia. In this he for the first time takes pains to create a certain public image. Initially, hypocrisy is a difficult game:

> How hard it is to be a hypocrite!
> At least to me who am but newly so.
> I thought it once a kind of knavery,
> Nay cowardice, to hide one's fault; but now
> The common frailty, love, becomes my shame
> He must not know I love the ungrateful still . . .
>
> [III, i]

Once fallen, he proceeds downward apace. His desire for Olivia as it is thwarted becomes increasingly difficult to bear, and he falls into greater and greater deceit in attempting to disguise it. His first lie to Freeman is merely the pretense that he is above feeling a woman's scorn. It is followed by his more serious attempts to deceive Fidelia, whom he would have believe that his various efforts to rape Olivia are designed not to satisfy himself but to punish her. But, finally, when he tells Vernish (before he knows him to be Olivia's husband) that he has enjoyed Olivia's favors, he reveals himself a finished hypocrite. This last falsehood is designed not to cover his shame but to boast in the hope of gaining another's admiration. It is an act of gratuitous hypocrisy. Hypocrisy for self-defense becomes hypocrisy for its own sake; and Wycherley, following the example of his Elizabethan predecessors, proves his satirist guilty of the very vice against which he rails.

In choosing lust as the vice which Manly's hypocrisy endeavors to disguise, Wycherley fulfills the last requirement demanded by the Elizabethan convention. This choice establishes beyond doubt that Wycherley was following Elizabethan satiric decorum, rather than Restoration dramatic decorum. The latter would classify Manly, because of his delight in combat, his courage, his cruel bravery, as the warrior type, or the hero of irregular greatness.[6] Animal lust and fierce courage are incompatible traits in a Restoration hero. Heroic honor demands heroic love; only when love is ennobling can it be the handmaiden of heroic courage. Lust, particularly the obscene lust of Manly and Olivia, which can in no wise be thought heroic, is a quality incongruent with courage in the Restoration view. On the other hand, lust combined with envy and sadism forms that complex of vices characteristic of the Elizabethan satyr-satirist. When we first encounter Manly, he declares that he is in

6. Cf. E. M. Waith, *The Herculean Hero* (London, 1962).

love with the only woman in the world whose honesty compares with his own. In Act II we find that his love for Olivia
is really self-love, for she has elicited it by imitating him.
Once Manly has been disenchanted, his love of Olivia turns
into a lust, as ungovernable as his rage, which grows more
intense as it is rebuffed. He sends the disguised Fidelia to sue
for him, and when she returns with Olivia's rejection and
the news that she herself has become the unwilling object
of Olivia's passion, Manly is thrown into a rage. His envy of
Fidelia's seductive qualities, of her ability to attract Olivia
when he cannot, leads him to wild outbursts of sadistic rage.

> Her love—a whore's, a witch's love!—But what, did
> she not kiss well, sir?—I'm sure I thought her lips—
> but I must not think of 'em more—but yet they are
> such I could still kiss—grow to—and then tear 'em off,
> . . . grind 'em into mammocks, and spit 'em into her
> cuckold's face.   [IV, i]

Rage, lust, envy, sadism—all the traits that mark the satyr-
satirist—are here in chaotic conflict. He is driven mad with
envy of Fidelia, whom he suspects of deceiving him with
Olivia, and of Olivia's husband, who has won her from him.
He is, however, unable to control his passion ("I must not
think of 'em more, but yet . . ."). And finally, these emotions
—unquenchable and inexpressible in action—find release
in a flood of wildly sadistic language.

In the last act Manly's character descends to the bestial
level. In an atmosphere sickeningly obscene the satyr's imprint beats out the last traces of the reformer. He goes with
Fidelia to Olivia's apartments. Hidden in the darkness, he
watches Olivia shamelessly pursue the terrified Fidelia and
hears her vent her hatred of him. The revelation that Olivia
is a female satyr in honorable lady's clothes draws from
Manly the comment, "a goat or a monkey were fitter for

thee [than a gallant]." Yet he does not recognize that in her lust she is his mirror image. Like Thersites, though he spies on the object of his satiric commentary and condemns her lust, he at the same instant lusts for her with an intensity that matches hers, and he envies Fidelia's position. His hatred of Olivia diminishes his desire for her not a jot. At last he formulates a plan, cruel, obscene, and cowardly, to rape Olivia while Fidelia, her supposed gallant, "talks love" to her and to bring a crew of spectators to share his pleasure in unmasking her.

The deterioration of Manly's character—which has a place, as we shall see, within the classical satiric structure—is accomplished wholly within the bounds of the Elizabethan convention. Taking advantage of the satyr-satirist's moral duplicity, Wycherley gives Manly the "public personality"[7] of the satirist-reformer—relentless hatred of vice and fearless courage in exposing it—and gives him the "private personality" of the satyr: primitive and ungovernable rage, lust and envy, and guilt of the vice he attacks in others. The downfall of Manly occurs as his private vices overwhelm his public virtues and he is overthrown when he is exposed as he had exposed others. Manly's character, then, brings to full flower a tradition that begins with the dawn of English literary history and lives, amended but unbroken, throughout the Medieval and Renaissance periods. Yet so well does Wycherley render the type that Manly has been mistaken for a Restoration beau.

In characterizing Horner, Wycherley, with amazing dexterity, employs both of the two types of satiric spokesmen differentiated by the Elizabethans. For his basic characterization he chooses the Elizabethan parasite-satirist. But he goes on to make use of the device that we observed in Marston: having his character assume the mask of the mal-

7. This definition of the public and private personalities of the satiric spokesman is Kernan's.

content-satirist to promote a hidden intrigue. At heart Horner is the parasite-satirist—the heir of Jonson's Buffone —who, to further his plan for enjoying the favors of "honorable" ladies, assumes the disguise of a eunuch who, as the consequence of his impotence, has all the characteristics of the malcontent-satirist—the heir of Jonson's Macilente.

Horner occupies a position in the design of *The Country Wife* somewhat different from the position Manly occupies in the design of *The Plain Dealer*. We shall consider this point more fully in discussing the structure of the two plays. Briefly, in the design of *The Plain Dealer* the satirist's persona is a character in the play. Manly is a grotesque caricature of the poet who writes satire in the same way that Macilente is a caricature of Asper. Horner occupies the position in *The Country Wife* that Buffone occupies in *Every Man Out*. His character is not a commentary upon the satirist as satirist, for in *The Country Wife* Wycherley is not questioning the value of satire itself. However, though Horner is not the satirist's persona, he is the spokesman of satire in the play; his comments underscore what is false and ridiculous in the scene. Yet even while his words and actions *are* exposing the other characters (and here is the significant point of difference), he does not intend such an exposure. His aim, like that of a Mosca or Buffone, is to exploit, rather than to expose or punish, the vices that he detects in others. Though he is sharply aware of the lust and hypocrisy that surround him, he is not detached from it, nor has he any inclination to be. He, too, is lustful; he, too, is a hypocrite. His desire is to make use of the lust and hypocrisy of others. He assumes the disguise of a malcontent-satirist who is repelled by lust with full appreciation of the rich comedy of his action. His disguise is a device to further his secret design of turning vice in others to his own enjoyment. The perfect parasite-satirist, Horner is sufficiently aware of the vice under consideration to ridicule it, but he uses it to satisfy his own pleasure. With beautiful irony, he chooses as his disguise the public image of the satirist—discontent, harshness of tone, railing at vice. In Manly, without his being aware of the change, the private personality of the satyr gradually overwhelms the public personality of the satirist. In Horner, the public personality of the satirist screens the machinations of the private personality, the satyr. And the clever parasite, fully conscious of his moral duplicity, revels in it.

In Horner's disguise the whole psychology of the malcontent-satirist that we have observed in Manly is expressed. Horner wants to convince the world that he is impotent. He pretends, therefore, to be discontent, harsh, brutally frank. He pretends that his aim is to injure women, lustful hypocrites, by exposing their hidden vices. He assumes to this mock end, speech that is both hostile and obscene. He counts upon his audience—Sir Jasper and the other guardians of chastity—to suppose the motivation of his abnormally cruel behavior, to suppose, that is, that his cruelty is bred of envy, and that his envy, in turn, results from his debarment by sexual injury from the natural pleasures of men. This is precisely the psychological syndrome of the malcontent-satirist, reversed. The malcontent-satirist, we will recall, is always by some means rendered impotent. He is either, like Thersites, a coward, or, like Macilente, a poor and ugly wretch, or, like Malevole, a man who has lost everything, or, like Manly, a primitive whose natural course of action is denied by civilized society. Impotence breeds envy and envy, rage, which can find satisfaction only in brutal language, a weapon to injure, ridicule, and expose the envied. Horner, familiar with the logic of this psychology, counts upon it to make his disguise credible. At one point, to ensure its impression upon the minds of those he wishes to deceive, he goes so far as to openly draw for their the impotence-envy-rage relationship.

> DORILANT: Did I ever think to see you keep company with women in vain.
> HORNER: In vain! no—'tis since I can't love 'em, to be revenged upon 'em.   [III, ii]

Women become the target of his pretended rage because they are associated with his pretended impotence. Just so, Ajax is the object of Thersites' railing because Thersites, rendered impotent by cowardice, would like to beat him but cannot.

Carefully constructing his disguise, Horner employs particularly the malcontent-satirist's method of injuring by giving scandal that will destroy his pretended victim's reputation:

> HARCOURT: . . . but do the ladies drink?
> HORNER: Yes sir; and I shall have the pleasure at least of lying 'em flat with a bottle, and bring as much scandal that way upon 'em as formerly t'other.   [III, ii]

His statement shows recognition of the complexity of his disguise. The satirist's aim in bringing scandal is vicarious action, the mere substitute for what he would do were he not by some means rendered unable.

In the company of those whom he particularly wishes to dupe, the tough guardians of his prey, Horner assumes to perfection the manner and tone of a malcontent-satirist.

> SIR JASPER: Come, come, man; what, avoid the sweet society of womankind? that sweet, soft, gentle, tame, noble creature, woman, made for man's companion—
> HORNER: So is that soft, gentle, tame, and more noble creature a spaniel, and has all their tricks; can fawn, lie down, suffer beating and fawn the more; barks at your friends when they come to see you, makes your

bed hard, gives you fleas and the mange sometimes.
And all the difference is, the spaniel's the more faithful
animal and fawns but upon one master.   [II, i]

Such a speech could be put without change into the mouth
of Manly, or even Macilente and be completely consistent
with their usual diction. It is with pointed subtlety that
Horner uses this public personality in the service of his
private self. In Act I, for example, his pretended intention
is to strip away the mask of virtue which Lady Fidget and
Mrs. Squeamish affect.

> LADY FIDGET: Foh! he's but too much a French fellow,
> such as hate women of quality and virtue for their love
> to their husbands . . . pray let us begone.
> HORNER: You do well, madam; for I have nothing
> that you came for. I have brought over not so much as
> a bawdy picture, no new postures, nor the second part
> of the *Ecole des Filles;* nor— . . . .
> LADY FIDGET: Ay! he's a base fellow . . . affectation
> makes not a woman more odious to them than virtue.
> HORNER: Because your virtue is your greatest affec-
> tation, madam.   [I, i]

Ironically, though it is not his aim, Horner does expose
bestiality hiding behind the mask of virtue in these women.
Ostensibly, he does so because he hates them and wills that
his exposure injure them. Actually, his reasons are two. In
the first place, this kind of attack strengthens his disguise;
harsh frankness and the desire to unmask sexual depravity
mark the malcontent-satirist. In the second place, he aims
to throw Sir Jasper off the scent by pretending disgust at the
very vice he means to enjoy. Wycherley's aim is larger still.
In such an attack Horner serves as satiric spokesman, for
what he says, regardless of why he says it, calls attention to
the moral imbalance in the scene presented us.

In his basic character, the parasite-satirist's, Horner's business is also to ferret out vice, but here he is working for himself, not for society. It is in part to detect hidden sexuality that he plays at being a eunuch, for, he says, "women of quality are so civil you can hardly distinguish love from good breeding, and a man is often mistaken, but now I can be sure she that shows an aversion to me, loves the sport." Once he has distinguished the ladies who "love the sport," however, he is as anxious as they that the illusion of their virtue be preserved, for it provides yet another screen for his operations. Still, though he promotes their hypocrisy and is indeed one of their number, being guilty of more enormous deception than they, he is yet sharply aware of their immorality. In fact, he is better able to differentiate between vice and virtue than a bitter satirist like Manly, because his motivating humour is not blind emotion but sharp-eyed interest. Further, though he is himself immoral, he values virtue as it appears, for instance, in Alithea and he is sorry when he believes that her virtue is to be thrown away upon a clod like Sparkish. At the end of the play his admiration of her virtue almost moves him to generous action. But, alas, her virtue is at odds with his interest, and the latter is the god he serves (the poet's vision has turned away from pastoral, where virtue cures self-interest, to satire, where virtue is lucky to preserve itself). However, when his interest is not endangered, Horner exhibits the keen perception of the satirist, even when it is not in the service of his disguise. He comments upon the immorality of Fidget and company in something of the style, though without the ferocity, of the satirist-reformer.

> Your bigots in honour are just like those in religion; they fear the eye of the world more than the eye of Heaven; and think there is no virtue, but railing at vice, and no sin, but giving scandal.   [IV, iii]

Like Buffone, however, he is careful to restrain his commentary until those he exploits are out of earshot, or, if he is moved to satire in their presence, he resorts to double entendre, which they are too self-absorbed to understand. When in Act V he is with his ladies of "honour" and finds himself in danger of losing their favor (for they have just discovered that he has played the same game with each of them), he expresses his opinion of the relative importance of "the eye of the world" and "the eye of Heaven" somewhat differently:

> LADY FIDGET: Well then, there's no remedy; sister sharers, let us not fall out but have a care of our honour. Though we get no presents, no jewels of him, we are savers of our honour . . . which shines yet to the world unsuspected, though it be counterfeit.
> HORNER: Nay, and is e'en as good as if it were true, provided the world think so; for honour, like beauty now, only depends on the opinions of others.   [V, iv]

True to Elizabethan convention, this parasite-satirist though cleverer and more keenly perceptive to moral issues than the other characters, is himself immoral. He ridicules the moral duplicity that surrounds him, but never when to do so would endanger his interest, which is to profit from the vice he observes.

The major difference between the bitter satirist, like Manly, and the parasite-satirist, like Horner, is that while the former is lacerated by the sight of vice, the latter is amused by it. Horner is rather more than less aware of vice than Manly, and can be as sharp in his criticism of it. But the world in all its corruption does not displease him. The tone of the parasite-satirist is, therefore, always closer to comedy than that of the malcontent-satirist. He ridicules but never bludgeons. Consequently, in Elizabethan practice the parasite-satirist became associated with a wittier satire, the

malcontent-satirist with a darker, more obscene satire. That
is not to suggest that the parasite-satirist is always comic,
like the clownish Buffone, or that his satire need not be as
pointed and skillful in exposing corruption as that of the
bitter satirist. Mosca is a parasite-satirist, yet *Volpone* is
hardly comic in tone. The malcontent-satirist paints corrupt
reality in all its blackness, describes in detail the fearful
mien of vice. The parasite-satirist employs wit to disclose
the moral incongruity in human life, but that incongruity
amuses him as well as his audience. He revels in the world
as it is. For this reason Horner does not occupy the central
position in this satire. He is too deeply involved in vice, too
much a part of the satiric scene to be the persona of the
satirist. However, Horner as spokesman allows more freedom to the real satirist, Wycherley. In him Wycherley makes
the best use of both parts of the Elizabethan convention. He
can be harshly satirical when he uses the disguised Horner as
his spokesman, wittily satirical when he uses the clever
parasite as his spokesman, and dramatically satirical when
he uses Horner as an instrument of satire, as a gigantic
emblem of the vice that concerns him in *The Country Wife.*
His versatility in the use of his inheritance from the Renaissance is almost endless; it makes him a worthy heir.

Part II. The Structure of the Satires: The Roman Voice

In his "Essay on Comedy" Meredith speaks of the three
traditions in comedy which alone are acceptable to the English: the Rabelaisian, the sentimental, and the satiric
"which smells of carrion." He argues the superiority to these
of French comedy:

> It may be shown by an analysis of Wycherley's *The
> Plain Dealer,* a coarse prose adaptation of *The Misan-
> thrope* stuffed with lumps of realism in a vulgarized

theme to hit the mark of English appetite, that we have
in it the keynote of the comedy of our stage. It is
Molière travestied, with hoof to his foot and hair on
the pointed tip of his ear.[8]

Meredith's argument need not concern us. It is as fruitless
to argue the superiority of French over English comedy as
it is to argue that an apple is better than a pear; they are
different. However, his observation of a difference between
French and English taste and his assertion that English
satire "smells of carrion" though extreme, is true for certain
periods. Bonamy Dobrée explains the distinction in saying
"French comedy aimed at an aesthetic result, English comedy
at being amusingly moral."[9] In general, until the Augustan
age, the English held intention above design in literature.
This very preference, as we have seen, motivated the development of the satyr-satirist figure.

Meredith's further observations, that Wycherley is full of
lumps of realism and that his theme, compared to Molière's,
is vulgar are accurate. It is unfortunate that he used these
observations as false evidence to support his private preference rather than as the basis for investigation of the nature
of the difference between the two poets. His suggestion that
Wycherley is Molière with cloven feet and hairy ears, though
untrue, hints that Meredith might, if he had pursued the
question further, have arrived at the reason for the difference
between the two poets. Essentially, the difference is that
Molière used satiric techniques in designing comedy, while
Wycherley used comic techniques in designing satire.
Wycherley's governing vision is different from Molière's. His
lumps of realism, his vulgarized theme, even his cloven foot
and hairy ear, are indicative of the genre in which he works.
Satire is of necessity the most realistic of the literary genres

8. George Meredith, "An Essay on Comedy," *Comedy*, ed. Wylie
Sypher (New York, 1956), p. 16.
9. Dobrée, p. 48.

because its subject is real social ill; its declared function is to cure social distemper. Its themes are perforce vulgarized because its method is to exaggerate human nature downward, that the audience may be shocked, indeed revolted, by the corruption to which, in their lives, they contribute. Wycherley probably borrowed some devices of Molière—the jealous husband unwittingly carrying his wife's letter to her lover, the jealous man leading his beloved to her gallant. But they are stock devices; Wycherley had used females in disguise being led by unwitting servants in *Love in a Wood*. He borrows more from Calderon in *The Gentleman Dancing Master* than he ever borrows from Molière. The point is that whatever devices he borrows, from whomever he borrows them, he puts to his own use. If he borrows comic devices of Molière, he uses them to the end of creating satire.

Molière's vision is comic. In his design he is concerned to present not the black-white vision of the satirist but the many aspects of reality. The Restoration playwright whose design most closely resembles Molière's is Etherege, not Wycherley. Molière's method, like Etherege's, is to throw into contrast many different views of life and to let the worth of each be tested against the others. For example, in *The Misanthrope* (with which *The Plain Dealer* is always compared) Molière places in juxtaposition the views of Alceste and Celimène, of Celimène and Eliante, of Celimène and Arsinoë, of Alceste and Philinte. These views are tested against one another. But Alceste's view, for instance, is not shown to be morally superior to that of Celimène. All the views of life have worth; all, except that of Arsinoë, are to some extent true and admirable. How different is this design from the satiric design of *The Plain Dealer*. Satire cannot afford ambiguity. In Wycherley's play Manly's deterioration is measured by the extent to which he finally deviates from his initial declared position. And the one good character in the play, Fidelia, embodies the virtue that Manly as reformer extols. Like all satire, *The Plain Dealer* has a moral view-point; it distinguishes between a right and a wrong way of life.

In addition to the difference between Wycherley's and Molière's designs is the difference between their conceptions of a central figure. Meredith unknowingly stumbled upon something when he mentioned the hooved foot and hairy ear. As we have seen, Manly bears the distinguishing characteristics of the English satyr-satirist. Compare such a creature with the urbane Alceste. Alceste is hardly even a misanthrope. He may hate the sin, but he is far too fond of the sinner. His affection for Philinte, his love of Celimène, his regard for the worth of Eliante disqualify him from the ranks of true haters of humanity like Manly. Folly irritates him, but it hardly drives him to the extremes of passion into which a real misanthrope like Manly is led. If we can imagine for an instant a scene so grotesque as Manly in the atmosphere of the French play, we can envision no actions congruent with his characterization except marriage to Arsinoë or rape upon Celimène. The vital difference between the protagonists of these plays is, of course, that their characters are determined by quite different designs. Alceste represents one view of reality, like all views partly true and partly false. So constructed, he fits perfectly the part determined for him by a comic scheme. Manly is a satiric spokesman. In his public personality he embodies virtue; in his private personality he shows how far from virtue human nature has fallen. Dobrée settled the question of Molière's influence upon Wycherley when he declared that Wycherley's comedy "was of English growth, that it would have existed substantially the same had Molière never lived."[1]

The French influence upon Wycherley, and indeed upon all Restoration and Augustan writers of satire, is far more complex and far less specific than the borrowing by one

1. Ibid., p. 57.

writer of another's techniques. It is not to Molière, the practitioner, that we must go, if we are to understand the French
influence upon Wycherley, but to Boileau, Bossu, Dacier,
to the seventeenth-century French critics who transmitted
to English satirists their new perception of the rules of ancient composition. French criticism touched to life a new
English aesthetic, and it is upon this aesthetic that Wycherley's perception of the form of ancient satire rests.

Renaissance aesthetics grow out of a Christian view of
the universe by which it is led to concern itself with surface
beauties—with ornamentation rather than architecture in
poetry. Drastically simplified, the basis of Renaissance theory
is that the force that governs apparent reality, God, is un-
knowable. His ways are mysterious, his order not within
the province of man's understanding. Apparent life is merely
a "veil of beautiful fictions,"[2] the unordered manifestation
of an order which cannot be known. Poetry imitates nature
—that is, imitates a surface—and, consequently, the surface
beauties of a poetic work are what give it value. Poetry may
approach nature in one of two ways. Either, realizing the
inadequacy of apparent nature, it must attempt to heighten
its beauty by ornamenting,[3] or, if it attempts to follow the
methods of nature, it must present ultimate truths disguised
in beautiful adornment. Daniello, whom Sidney among
other Elizabethan critics follows, admonishes poets to: "hide
their useful teachings under various fictions and fabulous
veils, as the physician covers bitter medicine with a sweet
coating."[4] These theories were responsible for the cult of
external form, of ornamentation, that dominated Italian
criticism and the Renaissance English criticism that so closely
followed it.

2. Cf. H. B. Charlton, *Castelvetro's Theory of Poetry* (Manchester,
   1913), pp. 27 ff.
3. Cf. Fracastro, *de Poetica,* 1.340.
4. Daniello, *Poetica* as quoted in Spingarn, *A History of Literary Criticism in the Renaissance* (New York, 1925), p. 20.

Theories of the imitation of nature become in time theories of the imitation of other poetry, masterworks. And, they, of course, guided the Renaissance approach to ancient literature. The theories of imitation of the Italians—Vida, Minturno, Scaliger—stress the borrowing of surface beauties—stylistic turns, tropes, sound effects:

> Italian Renaissance imitation of the classics resulted in the study and cult of external forms. Elegance, polish . . . became objects of study for themselves. . . . the intricacies of style and versification were carefully studied. Vida [laid] down laws of imitative harmony. Bembo, and after him Dolce and others studied the poetic effect of different sounds . . . the value of various vowels and consonants. . . . Later came the rhetorical treatises . . . and the more practical manuals.[5]

The Restoration is neither more nor less thorough, neither more nor less intense in its approach to the ancients than is the Renaissance. Their approaches differ only as their perceptions of the use to which ancient literature can be put are different. As the Renaissance view had been, the Restoration's view was determined by a perceptual set shaped by its philosophic outlook. Each period found in the ancients fulfillment of its own aesthetic needs. The initial impulse of the seventeenth century for a fresh appraisal of ancient thought came not from art, but from science. The new science, determined to tear away the veil of beautiful fictions, postulated that not mystery but a rationally perceptible order lay behind apparent nature. Moreover, it promoted the idea of man as a unit of reason, possessed of a sense that could best understand the abstract order when it was itself an abstract instrument. Thought and, consequently, methods of communication must be stripped of the accretions of custom, of superfluous ornamentation. The products of this

5. Spingarn, p. 126.

abstract thinking were abstract systems—of cosmology, of politics and, eventually, of literary criticism. The aesthetics that grew from such a view of the universe rested upon the principle, again, drastically simplified, that poetry was an ordered abstraction, constructed upon abstract, ordered principles the function of which was to reflect not surface reality, but the abstract metaphysical order beyond appearance. As the new philosophy called into doubt the old, so the new criticism rejected Renaissance theories of ornament and "the vicious abundance of phrase" to which those theories gave rise. It called for a literature whose "constant resolution would be to reject all amplifications, digressions and swellings of style, to return back to the primitive purity and shortness, when a man deliver'd so many *things* almost in an equal number of words."[6] Stripping language to its barest, essential form was, however, only a first step, really little more than a change in taste. The shift in aesthetic view had consequences far more comprehensive than this. If poetry is considered the formal reflection of metaphysical order, there must be rules governing its form as there are rules that determine the form of abstract nature. Consequently, poetic form and the theoretical rules that govern composition become the central obsession of Restoration criticism. Rules, the product of reason, shape form and it is in the form of poetry that its worth and beauty lie. Without rules "all must be governed by unruly fancy and poetry become the land of confusion which is, in reality, the kingdom of beauty, order, and harmony."[7]

To maintain its new aesthetic view, the Restoration had, of course, to reject Italian literary theory. It turned for guidance instead to French criticism. Moral intention had never

---

6. Thomas Sprat, "A History of the Royal Society," *Critical Essays of the Seventeenth Century,* ed. Spingarn, 2, 117–18.
7. Gildon, *The Complete Arte of Poetry,* Dialogue II, *Critical Essays of the Eighteenth Century,* ed. W. H. Durham (New Haven, 1915), p. 18.

obscured for the French, as it had for the English, the aesthetic demands of art. Even before the rise of neoclassicism, they were concerned with form. Their first experiments in satire exhibit the formalism of their approach. "Highly stylized, geometrically air-tight patterns were devised for half a dozen small preliminary satiric forms which served as fore-runners to the first formal verse satires of Du Bellay and Regnier."[8] When the scholarship of Casaubon (*De Satyrica Graecorum et Romanorum Satira*, 1605, which corrected the error of deriving satire from the satyr play) proved the inadequacy of Renaissance theories, the need arose for new consideration of Roman satire. Dacier stressed the obligation that critics were under to abandon the superficiality of the Renaissance and to penetrate the structure of the works.

> Hitherto we have been content to see only the outside; and 'tis a strange thing that Satyrs which have been read so long have been so little understood or explained; they have made a halt at the outside and were wholly busied in giving the interpretation of words.[9]

However, emphasis of the need to reconsider Roman satire is but the smallest part of the French contribution toward shaping English theories of satire. Had the French supplied no more than this, their influence could hardly have changed the course of English aesthetics and, consequently, could have affected English satire not at all. What the French provided was reason for the return not just to ancient practice but to ancient theory. In the minds of English critics, the French were held to be pioneers in showing that the order of the universe is to be found in the form of ancient

8. M. C. Randolph, "The Structural Design of Formal Verse Satire," *Philological Quarterly*, 21 (1941), 377.
9. Dacier, "An Essay upon Satyre," appended to *Bossu's Treatise of the Epike Poem* (London, 1719), p. 311.

poetry and that instruction in the means of recreating that order is to be found in ancient theory.

> Had Bossu never writ the world had still
> Like Indians viewed this wond'rous piece of Skill;
> As something of Divine, the work admired,
> Hoped not to be Instructed, but Inspired;
> Til he, disclosing sacred Mysteries,
> Has shown where all the mighty Magic lies,
> Described the Seeds, and in what order sown,
> That have to such a vast proportion grown.[1]

In this need for an abstract system of literary criticism to answer the demands of the new philosophic rationalism, the English valued the French for disclosing the design of ancient poetry and admired them for abstracting ancient rules. Even the methods and style of the French critics were prized, for as Gildon says, they "burden not our memories, nor confound our judgments by multiplicity of quotations (as Scaliger and our English men of learning do) but give us solid doctrine . . . They dwell not on mere words, but penetrate further into the reasons, sense and judgment of the ancient authors."[2]

However, somewhat ironically perhaps, the English view was that though the French had pointed the way toward revaluation of ancient thought, the English were better equipped to vitalize it anew. They identified themselves in particular with the Romans of the Augustan period, their notion being of Britain as the second Rome, deriving from but far out-stripping France, the second Greece.

> O may I live to hail the Glorious day,
> And sing loud Paeans through the crowded way,

---

1. John Sheffield, Earl of Mulgrave, *"An Essay upon Poetry,"* in *Critical Essays of the Seventeenth Century,* ed. Spingarn, 2, 296.
2. Gildon, as quoted by A. F. B. Clark, *Boileau and the French Classical Critics in England* (Paris, 1925), p. 235.

> When in Triumphant State the British Muse,
> True to herself, shall barb'rous aid Refuse,
> And in the Roman Majesty appear,
> Which none know better, and none come so near.[3]

Restoration criticism abruptly turns its back upon its native
English critical tradition; it firmly rejects the Christian view
of poetics and affects complete identification with Augustan
Rome. It looks shamefaced at its barbarous past as an aber-
ration from the true English destiny.

> I grant that from some Mossie Idol Oak
> In Double Rhymes our Thor and Woden spoke;
> And by Succession of Unlearned Times,
> As Bards began, so Monks Rung on the Chimes.
> But now that Phoebus and the Sacred Nine
> With all their Beames on our blest Island shine,
> Why should not we their ancient Rites restore,
> And be what Rome or Athens were Before?[4]

The new Restoration aesthetics, then, presented, at least to
the men who were involved in shaping it, a complete break
in the English tradition and the assumption of Augustan
Roman critical views. Rejecting the ways of the Renaissance,
the Restoration does not borrow from the ancients to bolster
its own theories. Rather it sees a resemblance between itself
and Augustan Rome, which resemblance it seeks to make
total by adopting wholesale not only the rules but also the
methods, approaches, and attitudes of Augustan Roman
literature.

Basic among these attitudes was the view that literary criticism and literary creation are closely allied arts. Poet and
critic are mutually dependent offices of the same man. Lucilius, Cicero, and Horace—to the Restoration, the giants upon

3. Roscommon, "An Essay on Translated Verse," *Critical Essays of the
Seventeenth Century*, 2, 309.
4. Ibid.

whose shoulders modern pigmies should strive to stand—
were equally eminent as creative artists and as literary critics.
Moreover, as poets they consciously based their creation upon
critical theories of craftsmanship.[5] The Restoration poet was
admonished to learn the rules of composition before he
essayed to employ them, to,

> With pains, and leisure, by such Precepts [Horatian] write
> And learn to use their arms before they fight.

The precepts themselves were, of course, to be sought in
Roman theory. The line of necessity is not hard to trace; Restoration philosophy calls for abstract order in art; Restoration aesthetics is led by way of French criticism to seek
Roman art as the embodiment of the abstract natural order.
Since the Roman artist was also the Roman critic, and since
Roman criticism stressed that the way to achieve order in
art was to first formulate rules of craftsmanship, Restoration
aesthetics are inevitably led to Roman critical theory. It goes
to Rome for the foundation of criticism itself, the formulation of an aesthetics. Consequently, the approach of the
Restoration to ancient works is itself directed by ancient
critical precepts. The basis of Restoration aesthetics rests
upon three interrelated Roman concepts, the theories: of
ideal form, of *unity embracing and controlling variety,* and
of the *imitation of ideal models.*

The theory of ideal form derives ultimately from Plato's
theory of Ideas, which postulates that there exists a perfect
abstract form of each thing, and that we judge things by the
degree in which they correspond or to which they approach
perfect form.[6] In the hands of Aristotle the theory of Ideas
is made to apply to aesthetics. In answer to Plato's objection

---

5. Cf. George Converse Fiske, *Lucilius and Horace: A Study in the
   Classical Theory of Imitation* (Madison, 1920), pp. 31 ff.
6. Roy K. Hack, "The Doctrine of Literary Forms," *Harvard Studies
   in Classical Philology,* 27 (Cambridge, Mass., 1916), pp. 51 ff.

to art as the imitation of an imitation, Aristotle conceives the theory of poetic forms. According to Aristotle, "Art imitates nature; the form joined to matter in the physical world is the same form that is expressed in the matter of art."[7] From the theory of poetic forms Aristotle goes on to derive the classification of poetic genres, a definition that is absolute:

> To each definition is attached a penalty, which operates as automatically as any other scientific law: if you attempt to disregard the "law" of gravity, you pay the penalty by falling; if you attempt to disregard the law of tragedy, you pay the penalty because what you have written will not be tragedy. Conversely, if you obey the law strictly, the result will be a tragedy and if you obey it perfectly, the result will be a perfect tragedy.[8]

The appeal to Restoration criticism of an aesthetics that springs from this kind of doctrine is obvious. However, Aristotle confines his theories to the realm of philosophic speculation. The Restoration sought instruction in implementing such a philosophy of art. This was provided by the more practical aesthetics of Rome. For the Romans literary criticism was more nearly associated with craftsmanship than with philosophical speculation. Their contribution was to render into practical terms the Platonic and Aristotelian theorizing. By this means they derived their concept of literary "kinds."

The doctrine of literary kinds is the work of Horace who, of all the Romans, exerted the most influence upon neoclassical thought. However, Horace was above all a practical critic (hence his appeal to the seventeenth century) and, conse-

7. Richard McKeon, "Literary Criticism and the Concept of Imitation in Antiquity," *Critics and Criticism,* ed. R. S. Crane (Chicago, 1952), p. 162.
8. Hack, pp. 55–56.

quently, the Aristotelian theory was meaningful to him only because its practical implications had already been deduced by Cicero. In *Orator* (2.7, 3.10) Cicero outlines the first principle of his doctrine, derived from Aristotle, "that there existed in nature, according to Plato's theory of 'ideas', an ideal form of eloquence, which was eternal, unchanging and objective in character, the absolute and perfect type, of which all forms of human eloquence were but imperfect copies."[9] This is the first rough statement of what was to become the most important concept in Roman criticism. From Cicero's formulation of an ideal eloquence and Aristotle's classification of poetic forms, Horace derives his theory of the genres, or literary kinds—the idea that there is an ideal form for each of the genres. The practical offshoots of the theory of ideal form are the interrelated twin theories of decorum and of *lex operis*. *Lex operis* means that not only is there an ideal form, but there is also an ideal method, that is, there are laws that govern the composition of each of the genres. The theory of decorum is, in effect, the realization of *lex operis*. The law of decorum dictates that style and design must be appropriate to the ideal form of the chosen genre. The final consequence is that "For every literary procedure ... for each genre there exists a law of perfect form."[1]

Horace's *lex operis* became the characteristic method of Roman criticism. The approach of the Romans was always to tabulate the various "kinds"—tragedy, epic, lyric, pastoral, satire—and to endeavor "to formulate the law of each, which law determined the characteristics to be exhibited by all who labored in the particular genre. In conformity with the law of Decorum each genre was marked off from the others as having a special character and rules of its own."[2]

9. J. W. H. Atkins, *Literary Criticism in Antiquity* (Cambridge, 1934), 2, 29.

1. Hack, p. 22.

2. John F. D'Alton, *Roman Literary Theory and Criticism* (London, 1931), p. 398.

The second of the three pillars of Roman criticism, the concept of unity embracing and controlling variety, arises of necessity from the doctrine of decorum. Decorum is bifocal; it keeps one eye upon the ideal form and the other upon the limitations of the real world. It must mediate "between the one and the many, between the ideal form or genus dicendi and the practice of forensic eloquence [in oratory] between the poet's ideal and his practice and . . . between the part and the whole."[3]

In practical terms this law results in Horace's demand for an organic structural unit. In the *Ars Poetica* he reiterates again and again the need for harmonious relation between the parts themselves and between the parts and the whole. Parts must be vitally connected, structurally related into a single organic whole, otherwise the resulting poem is meaningless. There can be no special effects, no brilliant but irrelevant turns, nothing extraneous to the needs of the *uni formae*. Nevertheless, for the form to assume flesh, for the structure to be an *organic* structure, the parts must have each a life of its own; they must vary. The resulting poem, then, equals variety in the service of unity. Quintilian's guide books to correct composition reduce Horace's theory to practical admonition. Insisting with Horace that style must grow naturally under the guidance of form (*Inst. or.* 8.21), Quintilian cautions that after the mode of expression has been determined there must be no hunting after words, no glaring "beauties," but rather all must be resolved in a single unity. He goes on to say that the poet will learn in time that structure and polish are not inconsistent with vigor, that, on the contrary, nothing can attain full strength without design—a unified, unifying structure.

The logical transition from the doctrines of ideal form

3. Mary Grant and George Converse Fiske, "Cicero's *Orator* and Horace's *Ars Poetica*," Harvard *Studies in Classical Philology*, 25 (1924), 17.

and decorum to the third mainstay of Roman criticism, the
doctrine of imitation, is inevitable. If there is an ideal form
in each genre, if decorum mediates between the ideal form
and the actual poem, then the *lex operis* must be derived
from an actual poem that comes closest to attaining ideal
form. For example, if there is a form in the world of ideas
for epic and if Homer's is the actual poem that in the phenomenal world comes closest to achieving that ideal, then
the lex operis for epic should be derived from Homer. Imitation of masterwork models is the compromise that the law
of decorum affects between the poet's desire to recreate a
pure, abstract ideal and the limiting necessity of his having
to use empirically observed pheomena in its creation.
Horace advocates imitation of Greek models, but the imitation must be of *their generically determined form,* their
structural design, since it is in form that they approach the
ideal. The Roman theory, then, is that *form* is the object of
imitation. Quintilian, again reducing theory to a practical
methodology, advocates imitation of classical models as natural (since art is nature methodized, 9.10.5) as well as expe-
dient. He is careful, however, to explain the nicety of judgment necessary in one who would imitate. The imitator must
first choose a congenial model (10.11.19), because to achieve
his true ends the imitator must identify with him whom he
imitates. In approaching his model, the imitator must bear
in mind that imitation is not a matter of borrowing words
or phrases (10.11.27). Rather, what is to be employed is
the method, the judgment, the arrangement—in short, the
structural design of the model.

The last among the ancients to contribute to the classical
theory of imitation was Longinus, who is for us especially
interesting, since he was not known to the Renaissance. The
first edition of *On the Sublime* did not appear until 1554
and at that time was largely ignored. It was not until the
seventeenth century, when the foremost neoclassical critic,

Boileau, introduced him, that European criticism felt the impact of Longinus. Longinus reiterates Horace's view of the importance of form in poetry, attacking those poets who claim to be possessed by divine frenzy. Nature works by method, he insists, and herself creates the system that art discloses. Following this line, he re-emphasizes the importance of unity. Sublimity is achieved in the choice and combination of details in an organic whole (C.10).[4] Imitation, then, he says, following Quintilian, requires identification of the imitator with his master. Identification by illuminating the spirit of the model will lead the imitator in the steps of his master's approach to ideal form.

> Accordingly, it is well that we ourselves also, when elaborating anything which requires lofty expression and elevated conception, should shape some idea in our minds as to how perchance Homer would have said this very thing, or how it would have been raised to the sublime by Plato or Demosthenes. . . . For those personages presenting themselves to us and inflaming our ardour and as it were illuminating our path will carry our minds in a mysterious way to the high standards of sublimity which are imaged within us.   [14.1]

Identification with the shaping spirit of a master poet leads inevitably to the imitation of ideal form. It is not the work, but the way of his great predecessors that the imitator borrows.

These Roman principles as well as the attitudes toward literature that arise from them were adopted wholesale and formed the foundation of Restoration criticism. The rockbed upon which Restoration theory and practice rest is the principle of formal unity and the supporting principle of the imitation of generic form in classical models, an imita-

4. "Longinus" as quoted by T. R. Henn, *Longinus and English Criticism* (Cambridge, 1934), p. 92.

tion that is achieved by means of identification with the spirit of one's model. Unity of form is, of course, the central dictum. The parts, the beauties that were so highly prized by the Renaissance are in the eyes of the Restoration a vulgar necessity. "Number, and Rhyme, and that harmonious sound, Which never does the Ear with harshness wound are necessary, yet but vulgar Arts For all in vain, these superficial parts Contribute to the structure of the whole."[5] Sounds must not wound the ear but must guide it to an appreciation of the whole; figures must not be lozenges whose sweetness is individually savored. No part must call attention to itself but rather their variety must contribute to illuminate the unity which it serves, for it is in structural design, in form, that a work of art reflects the universal order. Structure is the reason and the soul of a composition.

> On sure Foundations let your Fabrick Rise,
> And with attractive Majesty surprise,
> Not by affected, meretricious Arts,
> But strict Harmonious Symetry of Parts,
> Which through the Whole insensibly must pass,
> With vital Heat to Animate the Mass.[6]

As the formalism—high regard for symmetry and unity of design—dictated by Roman theory determined the Restoration poet's perception of ancient literature, so Roman concepts of imitation directed the Restoration poet's way with his model. His choice of a model was made upon the evaluation of how well form realizes idea in it; his method was then to abstract and imitate that form. However, the medium through which he chose to realize the design of his model need not have resembled the medium of the original. Thus Dryden in his preface to *The State of Innocence* first explains

5. Mulgrave, "Essay on Poetry," Spingarn, *Critical Essays of the Seventeenth Century*, 2, 286.
6. Roscommon, "Essay on Translated Verse," ibid., 301.

that Milton's poem gives universal pleasure because in it thought is perfectly realized in a unified design and then defends his own medium as appropriate to the imitation of that design.[7] The Restoration conception of imitation, then, is determined (1) by the adoption without revision of Roman critical theory, which called for structural unity and the imitation of ideal literary models, and (2) by the new appreciation, in the light of these principles, of the form, structural unity and appropriateness of form to thought in ancient works themselves.

Accompanying, and indeed hastening, the change in the concept of imitation is a new theory of translation. Throughout the seventeenth century the direction taken by translators had been away from exact representation toward greater and greater freedom with the original. Cowley was thought to be the initiator of the method, but he was not singular in calling for a revolt from the slavish methods of translation of the Renaissance. "This way of leaving Verbal Translations and chiefly regarding the Sense and Genius of the Author was scarce heard of in England before this present age."[8] By the Restoration period translation is concerned solely with the spirit of the original; close following is thought to be detrimental to proper translation. Obviously, the new theories of translation, as well as the newly adopted Roman formalism, are part of a desire, necessitated by the philosophy of the age, to strip away all accretions and to render as sharply as possible the abstract essence of thought. Translators sought to penetrate beyond mere words to the "genius" of their chosen authors.

> Nothing checks and deadens the fancy more than a too superstitious respect for the original, especially in Poetry; it is commonly the cause that an idolatrous translation endeavoring too exactly to render all the beauties

7. Dryden, preface to *The State of Innocence*, in *Works*, ed. Summers.
8. Sprat, from "The Life of Cowley," Spingarn, 2, 132.

of his author gives you in truth never a one. Every
minute circumstance of thought cannot be preserved
with any tolerable grace, nor is it indeed necessary;
provided that the translator makes amends for his ne-
glect of what is less important by improving and if
possible refining upon essentials, which is better done
by studying the Genius . . . of the author.[9]

To the Restoration translator those "beauties" that were the
very plunder of the Renaissance imitator are superfluous
ornaments. What concerns the Restoration translator is the
"genius" of the work, that which renders the perfect forms
of nature into art. Translation, then, sought to abstract and
recreate in modern dress the essence of the work with which
it engaged. The imitator went still a stage further. He sought
an identification with the chosen author so close that he himself might conceive the generic form of the work. In his
preface to *The Fables* Dryden distinguishes between meta-
phrase, the slavish copying of Jonson and his followers,
paraphrase, the attempt to render the sense and spirit of the
original in modern dress, and imitation, the abstraction of
the form of the model and its adaptation to modern use.[1]

Imitation in its fullest development, then, became a kind
of original rendering of the model. The imitator identifies
so closely with his master that he becomes, as Roscommon
puts it "no longer his Interpreter, but He." The consequence
of this kind of identification is that it leads the imitator not
to copying but to emulation and, as a result, to revitalization
of the model. Denham praises this ability in Cowley:

> To him no author was unknown
> Yet what he wrote was all his own

9. Ozell, dedication to his translation of *Le Lutrin,* quoted by A. F. B.
Clark, p. 171.
1. Dryden, preface to *The Fables, Essays of John Dryden,* ed. Ker, 2,
252.

He melted not the ancient Gold
Nor with Ben Jonson did make bold
To plunder all the Roman stores
Of poets and of Orators
Horace's wit and Virgil's state
He did not steal, but emulate
And when he would like them appear
Their garb but not their Cloaths did wear.[2]

The method was especially favored by writers of satire, for they could achieve identification not merely between themselves and the ancient Roman poets whom they would imitate but between their age and the Augustan Age in Rome. Licentiousness, newfangledness, and the moral enervation they bred met them on the one hand, and "enthusiasm," the fervor of the wrong-headed, met them on the other. The atmosphere was comparable, the subject matter universal. Their method, then, was to employ the "genius" of the master-poet upon their own circumstances. Oldham explains the nature of his approach to ancient satire in this way:

> I fell to thinking of some course whereby I might serve myself of the Advantage which those that went before me [the Elizabethans] have either not minded, or scrupulously abridged themselves of. This I imagined to be effected by putting Horace into more modern dress than hitherto he has appeared in, that is, by making him speak as if he were living and writing now.[3]

Whereas the Renaissance satirist borrowed the voice of his model, Juvenal, the Restoration satirist borrows the genius of his model and provides him with a new, Restoration voice.

After identification with the master, however, seven-

2. Denham, "On Abraham Cowley," as quoted by Elizabeth Nitchie, "Longinus and the Theory of Poetic Imitation in 17th and 18th Century England," *Studies in Philology*, 32 (1935), 588.
3. Oldham, advertisement to *Some New Pieces* (London, 1681), al^{r-v}.

teenth-century imitation required the perception by the imitator of the ideal, generic form to whatever extent it is realized in the model, i.e. the perception of the model's organic
design. The form was then abstracted from the model and
used as the framework of original composition. Most of the
satires in Boileau's 1666 edition are imitations of Horace
and Juvenal. They are not modernized translations, nor are
they paraphrases, but rather they are original poems with
Latin precedent behind them. When the design of one model
seems to him more nearly to realize ideal form than another,
Boileau feels free to dispense with it, or to diverge from one
to another model. Before his eyes always is the ideal form of
satire.

Adopting Roman rules and developing new methods of
translation and imitation profoundly affected the Restoration's wholly new conception of satire. In the first place,
identifying themselves with Rome caused them to prize more
highly the satiric mode itself—"Satire is all our own," Quintilian had said. But, more important, for the first time in
English literary history, satire was recognized as a generic
form having definable rules for the government of its composition. In true Roman style the most skillful Restoration
practitioner of the art of satire was also the foremost critic
of his age, and among the handful of critics in English who
have dealt with satire as a form.

> John Dryden was the first and remains almost the only
> English man of letters to have considered critically the
> matter of the architectural pattern of formal verse satire
> and then only in 1692/3 when England's first period
> of verse satire had long gone by and a second greater
> one even then underway.[4]

"A Discourse Concerning the Original and Progress of

4. Randolph, "The Structural Design," *Philological Quarterly* (1941),
   p. 380.

Satire" is a landmark in English criticism, for it records the abandonment of Renaissance notions of pristine irregularity in favor of the new conception which demanded in satire as in other modes a generically determined form, a unified design, a style, correct and easy, that subordinates variety to the service of unity. The moral function of satire was not forgotten; as Dryden insists, "Satyre lashes Vice into Reformation," but even morality itself is conceived of in formal terms. For example, when, at one point, Dryden criticizes Juvenal for having in the *Sixth Satire* "almost forgotten that he is now setting in for a moral poet," it is with Juvenal's form, not his intention, that he quarrels. In this satire, he says, Juvenal has not obeyed the formal requirement to present, as well as the condemnation of one principal vice, the recommendation of its opposing virtue. Dryden is concerned only with the formal requirements that bind one who sets up for a "moral poet." Freed from its false mythic origins and from its associations with righteously indignant religious reformers, satire could at last be considered an artistic form the discipline of which is determined by rules of composition.

Dryden's declaration of intention itself provides clear evidence of the new Restoration perception of satire. As satire is a recognizable genre, the manifestation of some ideal form, it must be possible to trace the development of the genre, to mark the contributions of its originators to the achievement of the form. He is unconcerned with the possible motivation of its originators. He has abandoned the superficiality that arrested the attention of the Renaissance at words; he has shaken off the prejudices that frightened Renaissance satirists into thinking Roman satire formless—

> riddle-like, obscuring their intent . . .
> the Roman ancients
> Whose words were short and darksome was
> their sense.
> Who reads one line of their sharp poesies

> Thrice must take his winde, and breathe
> him thrice.[5]

So said the Renaissance poet who boasted himself the first English satirist. How different is Dryden's view. His eye is upon the object; his purpose to call to his reader's attention the architecture, the generic form of satire that they, understanding that form, may use it. His examination, like Horace's investigation of Greek models, is prompted by practical considerations. He would derive from the theory of ancient writers the rules of satire.

> I tell you my own trivial thoughts how a modern satire should be made. I will not deviate in the least from the precepts and examples of the ancients who were always our best masters. I will only illustrate them and discover some of the hidden beauties in their designs, that we may thereby form our own in imitation of them.[6]

Dryden's purpose in writing the essay, then, is to abstract the form of satire. Closely following Roman principles, he postulates first that the subject of a satire is the examination of a single vice and recommendation of its opposing virtue. The basic satiric design is twofold: it exposes and proposes. Persius is praised for his unfailing adherence to this most fundamental structural division, for he is "never wanting in some profitable doctrine and exposing the opposite vices to it." Building the design that must rise from this basic foundation, Dryden cautions, requires strict observation of formal unity.

> This is the important secret in the designing of a perfect satire—that it ought only to treat of one subject, to be

5. Hall, Prologue to Book III, *Virgidemiarium, Complete Poems,* ed. A. B. Grosart (Manchester, 1879).
6. Dryden, "A Discourse Concerning the Original and Progress of Satire," *Essays,* ed. Ker, 2, 102.

confined to one particular theme; or at least to one principally. If other vices occur in the management of the chief they should be only transiently lashed and not insisted upon, so as to make the design double.[7]

The very use of the words "designing a perfect satire" is evidence of the revolution that has occurred. Satire is no longer an outburst, it is an artifice. Moreover, it is an artifice the perfection of which can be measured against some ideal form, and what is more, can be constructed in accordance with some abstract, ordered principle. It attacks vice not out of the need of some outraged satyr to give vent to his emotions, but out of the need of a predetermined formal design. In like manner, it recommends virtue not because Heaven cries out for virtue but because principles of construction do. The poet writing satire is responsible above all to a design. "Other virtues, subordinate to the first, may be recommended under that chief head; and other vices and follies may be scourged, besides that which he principally intends. But he is chiefly to inculcate one virtue, and insist on that." Having dealt with two of the three mainstays of Roman aesthetics, i.e. appropriateness of subject to mode and unity of form, Dryden goes on, in the footsteps of Horace, to consider the third, the subordination and control of variety within a unified whole. From the logic of his argument it is clear that he has the Horatian concept of decorum (as the mediator between the one and the many, the parts and the whole) in mind. The variety of the phenomenal world as well as the variety of the possible models available confronts the poet. But he must choose always with his eye upon the requirements of the ideal form as well as the restrictions of the design he has chosen.

> That variety, which is not to be found in any one satire, is at least in many written on several occasions.

7. Ibid.

> And if variety be of absolute necessity in every one
> of them, according to the etymology of the word, yet
> it may arise naturally from one subject, as it is diversely
> treated in the several subordinate branches of it, all
> relating to the chief. It may be illustrated accordingly
> with variety of examples in the subdivisions of it and
> with as many precepts as there are members of it.[8]

Variety has no value in itself, as it had had in the Renaissance, but is useful as it serves the ends of a unified structural
whole.

Dryden's essay is an essay in form. He ranges the progress
of satire to the end of disclosing its form; he marks the contributions of Lucilius, Horace, Juvenal, and Persius as they
are developments of that form. And all this is done to the
achievement of his final end, which is to uncover the *lex
operis* for satire. The essay was, of course, written in 1692,
well after the classical period in English satire was under
way. A full critical appraisal of the new view, it nevertheless
came, as most critical statements do, after the fact. Dryden's
own practice shows that he had put the rules to work long
before he catalogued them. If we compare Renaissance with
Restoration practice the difference between the two periods
in the form of satire as well as the method of imitation is
readily apparent. Consider the form, for example, of
Donne's[9] *Satyre I,* which borrows from Horace the device
of the "friend" calling upon the satiric spokesman to drag
him abroad. Upon the walk they encounter the objects of
satire and the "friend" leaves the satiric spokesman for the
company of another. But abandoning one's friend for the
company of another (one kind of hypocrisy found in *The*

8. Ibid., pp. 103–04.
9. I have chosen Donne, rather than Marston or Hall, because his tone,
   not so extreme as theirs, approaches the tone of Restoration satire.
   We are therefore left free in making this comparison to concentrate
   upon differences in formal structure.

Plain Dealer) is not illustrative of a central vice. The walk as well as the abandoning are situational rather than thematic effects and merely provide a loose framework in which countless vices, thought to be suitable targets of satire, are attacked—lust, hypocrisy, social climbing, ignorance, rudeness, etc. None of the vices is relevant to, much less subordinate to another. Here and there a situation or a figure is borrowed from Juvenal or Horace but parts are related neither to each other nor to the whole. *Satyre II* begins with what looks like a declaration of theme—there is one thing that I hate above all others in this town—but the poet is at once sidetracked into a digression on the folly of writing poetry. This digression ends with the observation that poetry is not a strong enough weapon against vice and, without any transition, the satiric persona turns his eye upon a new folly. The most distinctive quality of this satire is the irregularity of its form. The focus zig-zags from theme to theme—for example, in the middle of an attack on plagiarism an irrelevant digression on the sexual perversion of poets appears. The poem is without formal coherence, much less symmetry. This is quite the opposite method to the Restoration poet's glancing from aspect to aspect of the same vice. Obviously the Renaissance conceptions of roughness and irregularity are at work here. Donne occasionally catches the tone of Juvenal but he is either not aware of, or consciously ignores, the structure of ancient satire.[1] As an example of the Renaissance's method of borrowing we may take Hall. A fair num-

---

1. N. J. C. Andreasen, "Donne's Satyres," *Studies in English Literature*, 3 (1963), 59–76, in arguing the unity of Donne's satires supports my point. The satires, as he shows, are not each limited to the treatment of a single vice (as Restoration form would demand). Rather, all five satires are loosely organized around the "over-all thematic purpose of defending spiritual values against creeping materialism . . . " (p. 61). Donne's unity, in keeping with Renaissance satiric decorum, rests upon (1) the "personality" of the satiric spokesman, and (2) the recurrence of key images. It does not depend, as Restoration satire does, upon structural design.

ber of the *Virgidemiae* contain passages of Latin satire, but
they are used as effects in a typically irregular Elizabethan
structure. The first sixty lines of Book IV, *Satire 3,* for example, are imitative of parts of Juvenal's *Sixth Satire,* but
they provide merely a series of examples, parts to fit into
the string of parts that constitutes an Elizabethan satire.

Contrast with this Rochester's *Satyr against Mankind,* an
imitation in the Restoration sense of Boileau's *Eighth Satire.*
Rochester takes Boileau's theme and not only reembodies
it but recreates it in a new spirit. He imitates Boileau in the
very way that Boileau is imitating Latin satire. Rochester,
while he alludes to subordinate vices, never loses sight of
his main theme, that false reason is to be despised. When
he does attack other vices—man's inhumanity, the betrayal
of friendship by hypocrisy, cruelty that is prompted by the
mere wanton urge to destroy—he does so always with relation to his main theme. These are the "members" of the
central vice of which Dryden speaks, for Rochester uses
them only to prove the defectiveness of reason by making
a comparison between human and animal nature. Moreover,
obeying the classical precept, Rochester recommends the
virtue opposite to false reason, right reason

> Thus whilst against false Reas'ning I
> enveigh
> I own right Reason, which I would obey.[2]

The good, as in ancient satire, is plain, unadorned common
sense, the evil the new-fangled cult of rationality. Even in
Tunbridge Wells, where Rochester uses a structure that, like
Donne's in *Satyre I,* is situational, he is careful to maintain
thematic unity. Though in a parade of figures each exhibits
his own kind of folly, their follies are structurally related.
In Donne each of the figures provides the satiric spokesman

2. Rochester, "A Satyr against Mankind," *Works,* ed. John Hayward
(London, 1926), p. 38.

with a new subject. In Rochester the central vice though variously manifested in Sir Nicholas Cully's outrageously bad taste, in the pseudo-Spaniard's gravity when he buys eggs, in the elevated diction of the would-be fop and his female counterpart that degenerates to slang under stress, it remains the same vice, affectation that masks mediocrity, or beastliness. After he has called the variations upon the vice to our attention in the scene he presents, Rochester underscores their central relation in an open declaration of theme.

> So the Bear Garden Ape, on his Steed mounted
> No longer is a Jack-A-Napes Accounted
> But is, by virtue of his Trumpery then
> Called by the Name of a young Gentleman.
> Bless me! I thought, what Thing is man
>   that thus
> In all his Shapes is so ridiculous?
> Ourselves with Noise of Reason we do please
> In vain, Humanity's our worst disease.
> Thrice happy Beasts are, who because they be
> Of Reason void, are so of Foppery.[3]

We may note that Rochester's theme here is that which will become the central theme of Swift. Man is not merely beastly, but vain, proud, affecting the superiority of reason in his viciousness.

For the Restoration poet, then, satire is a form, a stern Muse whose discipline requires the poet to seek examples in the phenomenal world with which he may clothe in flesh an abstract ideal. Some poets acknowledge openly that they write in answer to the demands of a taxing genre.

> Satyr's my only province and delight
> For whose dear sake alone I've vow'd to write:

3. Rochester, "Tunbridge Wells," *Works*, p. 125–6.

> For this I seek occasion, court abuse,
> To show my parts and signalize my muse.[4]

Most poets, however, demonstrate in their works themselves the new perception of classical form, the new adherence to classical precept. Among these latter was Wycherley who admonishes us, with an ironic grin, to look to his play if we want evidence that he understands the rules:

> I can hardly keep myself from quoting Aristotle and Horace, and talking to you of the rules of writing (like the French authors), to show you and my reader I understand 'em in my epistle, lest neither of you should find it out by the play.[5]

By the time that Dryden's essay appeared Wycherley was universally acknowledged a master of the art whose rules it describes. Indeed Dryden assumes his reader to be so familiar with Wycherley's satire that he may use Wycherley to illustrate a characteristic of Juvenal.

> Juvenal is a more vigorous and masculine wit [than Horace], he drives his reader along with him. . . . When he gives over it is a sign the subject is exhausted and the wit of man can carry it no further. If a fault can justly be found in him, it is that he is too luxuriant, too redundant, says more than he needs, like my friend, The Plain Dealer, but never more than pleases.[6]

Dryden's essay, the verse satires of Rochester and Oldham, the last plays of Wycherley—all are fruits of the same neoclassical movement. All manifest clearly the Restoration's

---

4. Oldham, "Upon a Printer," quoted by C. W. Previté-Orton, *Cambridge History of English Literature, 8,* 82.
5. Wycherley, "Epistle Dedicatory" to *The Plain Dealer, William Wycherley,* ed. W. C. Ward (London, 1888), p. 370.
6. Dryden, *Essays, 2,* 84–85.

reappraisal and employment of the structural design of classical satire.

Let us follow their example, now, and for the purpose of clarification abstract the classical structural design. Reduced to simplest terms, the classical satiric design is bipartite. It breaks into two markedly disproportionate divisions, the thesis, which consists of an attack upon some specific vice or folly, and the antithesis, which recommends the opposing virtue. In the thesis the vice under consideration is considered in all aspects and attacked from as many angles as possible "in something of the way the premises are turned about in the octave of a sonnet."[7] The antithesis, by far the weaker of the two arguments, is usually presented as struggling hopelessly and helplessly against the forces described in the thesis. "Often the admonition to virtue . . . is only implied . . . But it is there, it must be there if the piece is to be more than mere virulence and fleeting invective."[8] The thesis and antithesis are the minimal essential for the classical design. The form that this essential assumes is this: an outer framework encloses thesis and antithesis. In it are the satiric spokesman and the adversarius, a kind of combative hollow man. The adversarius may be a stubborn mentor, a shadowy figure or even "you" understood. He may be an irrational member of the very group under attack who detaches himself from them to draw near the satirist. He can even be the dramatic representation of an actual person, as Pope's adversarius is in the *Epistle to Arbuthnot*. In rare instances, as in Juvenal's *Tenth Satire* the "friend" becomes the satiric spokesman while "the poet" assumes the adversarius' persona. The adversarius' function is to draw the satirist's fire. He may either bait the satirist, with questions or barbed rejoinders, or he may continually caution him against being too outspoken. Both devices are designed to draw comment and anecdote

7. Randolph, "The Structural Design," p. 369.
8. Ibid.

from the satirist. The two figures, satirist and adversarius, talk against a background—not infrequently a moving background—a street in Rome, a royal court, or, as in *The Plain Dealer,* Westminster Hall. The setting must be such that it allows a stream of figures to pass by upon whom the satirist can comment to the adversarius, and who will serve as proof of the satirist's contention that human nature has been corrupted by the vice in question. (Rochester's *Tunbridge Wells* provides an especially good "background" in its satiric design.) The satiric spokesman uses miniature dramas, vignettes, "characters" to push forward his argument, and by means of these miniature dramas and anecdotes still another "background" is provided. "Background" as it is used here signifies the scene presented (either in the words of the satiric spokesman or in the situation provided by the poet who writes the satire) as proof that reality is corrupt. The satiric spokesman and adversarius are set within a scene of corruption, and their discourse provides additional scenes of corruption. The three pillars of the satiric design then are: (1) a thesis to be argued, (2) a satiric spokesman and adversarius to argue it, and (3) a background to illustrate the truth of the satiric spokesman's position. The argument is invariably an indictment of human nature, for the satirist exaggerates downward to achieve his effects. Man appears in satire at his most gross and beastly.

The positive argument, whether stated or implied, is always the traditionally accepted idea of good, "differentiated in satire from the forms it might take in, say, lyric, by being viewed from the angle of social solidarity, rather than private introspection."[9] The good of the satirist is always plain, old-fashioned virtue—Juvenal's heroes are his primitive, acorn-belching ancestors. The evil of the satirist is the modern indulgence in vice that weakens his people as a nation, or

9. Mack, "The Muse of Satire," in *Studies in the Literature of the Augustan Age,* ed. Boys, p. 224.

as a level of society. It is the refusal of his own age to recognize sin as sin.

Wycherley's *The Plain Dealer* fulfills in every detail the structure outlined above. In addition to the tri-elemental structure of satirist-adversarius-background, it contains a parody substructure, so that it is at once a satire and a satiric questioning of satire itself. Since, in part for parody's sake, the classical satiric design is so boldly emphasized in this play, we shall violate chronology and consider it first, so that our discussion here will provide a background for our discussion of *The Country Wife*.

The play begins, as formal satire must, with a crashing declaration of theme. The vice under attack is hypocrisy. It is ubiquitous, for even the plain-dealer who attacks or tries to flee from it is in constant danger of being overtaken. The thesis is declared both verbally and situationally—that is, in Manly's spoken rebuke of Lord Plausible, as well as in the dramatic arrangement in which Manly, the plain-dealer, is pursued by Lord Plausible, the personification of hypocrisy. Manly, the satirist, lashes out at his target but finds that he is fighting a shadow; the more fierce his attack, the more elaborate the flattery it arouses from Lord Plausible.

The thesis declared, Wycherley sets the traditional contestants to argue it. There has been much critical speculation about the relationship between the characters in this play. Are we, with Dobrée, to consider Manly a hero and Freeman an opportunist, or are we to follow the more recent view, Holland's, which considers Manly "neurotic" and Freeman and Olivia "well-adjusted"? Does Freeman represent a sane and sensible virtue against which we are to measure Manly's excesses? Are Freeman and Eliza the touchstones upon which we are to measure the other characters in the play? When we recognize the play as formal satire, Freeman's role at once becomes clear: he is the adversarius. His function is to take a position opposite that of the satirist, Manly, and to provoke the satirist's attack. As we have seen, the adversarius may assume any of a number of shapes. Freeman's is a type quite common in Roman satire. He is one of the very number whom the satirist scorns. But he detaches himself from the crowd and draws near the satirist where he plays the role of devil's advocate. Freeman is not on the side of virtue. He does not want to convince Manly that the world is not really full of hypocrites, but rather he champions the position that hypocrisy is the way of the world, the means to success. He hopes, in effect, to reason the satirist to the side of unreason, to win him to the very vice he stands most firmly against. At the end of the play Freeman's behavior may seem inconsistent with his character (why should he, a hypocrite, tell Manly what he really thinks?). But we must keep in mind that the adversarius need not be consistent to fill his place in the satiric design. All that is required is that he maintain a position opposite to that of the satirist.

The relationship of Manly to Freeman is established in the first act, almost as soon as the play begins. Manly enters upon the scene first, and by the ferocity of his speech and manner declares himself the fearless satirist who is determined to expose hypocrisy to shame wherever he finds it. He begins his mission by cursing Lord Plausible for a "common whore or pickpocket, dangerous to those he embraces" and throwing him out of doors. He declares himself the champion of truth and the implacable enemy of the world and all its vanities. In fine, Manly proves himself possessed of the distinguishing characteristics of an Elizabethan satirist. Once Manly is so identified, the adversarius is permitted to enter. Freeman, as his name implies, is the Restoration *honnête homme;* in an Etheregean play he would be hero. He is a self-acknowledged opportunist who gets along with the world and whose sole motivation is self-interest. He cannot understand the disappointed idealism that makes Manly such a wildly misanthropic champion of truth. But since friendship is easy for him, he offers to be Manly's friend. Manly rejects his offer and thereby provides the point upon which their basically antagonistic views of life can be revealed, and their roles in the satiric design clearly laid down.

> MANLY: . . . you must pardon me, I cannot wish well to pimps, flatterers, detractors, and cowards, stiff nodding knaves, and supple, pliant, kissing fools. Now all these I have seen you use like the dearest friends in the world.
>
> FREEMAN: Ha!Ha!Ha! What, you observed me, I warrant, in the galleries at Whitehall, doing the business of the place? Pshaw! Court-professions, like court promises, go for nothing, man. But, faith, could you think I was a friend to all those I hugged, kissed, flattered, bowed to? Ha! Ha!
>
> MANLY: You told 'em so and swore it too; I heard you.
>
> FREEMAN: Ay, but when their backs were turned, did not I tell you they were rogues, villains, rascals whom I despised and hated? . . . Why don't you know, good captain, that telling truth is a quality as prejudicial to a man that would thrive in the world, as square play to a cheat, or true love to a whore?   [I, i]

That Freeman is openly an opportunist, that he acknowledges his resemblance to cheats and whores, makes him a more complex hypocrite than Plausible, but he is no more virtuous. It is necessary to the satiric design that he openly advocate the vice under consideration, since he and Manly must defend opposing views of good. To fulfill the satiric design, they must further be set to argue their views of the thesis against a background from which the satirist may draw examples to justify his position. Moreover, their discourse itself must supply background (used here in the special sense defined above) for the satirist's position.

In Act I Wycherley closely adheres to the limitations of
verse satire; he does not take advantage of the extra freedom
afforded him by the dramatic mode until he has laid a strong
foundation for the formal satiric structure. Having established the necessary antagonism between the satiric spokesman, Manly, and the adversarius, Freeman, he proceeds to
unfold the satiric background in the conversation of the
adversaries, for the moment following the mode of verse
satire. If we examine one of the key Act I exchanges between
Manly and Freeman we find that it is a formal satire in little;
that it not only employs the devices used in classical verse
satire but it sketches in miniature the satiric structural design.
Freeman provokes Manly with an argument that he knows
will draw his fury—that "everybody does it so it must be
right." Then Manly launches his counterargument. To illustrate that his hatred and disgust for the world are rational, he
describes a scene which is the usual crowded, moving "background" of formal satire. He caricatures the hypocrites of
the world in all their folly falling upon every level of society
from bishop to fishmonger. And finally this small satire
within a satire is clinched by a recapitulation of the fundamental disagreement of the two antagonists. Freeman begins
the exchange with a defense of his behavior as the mere
recognition and acceptance of the facts of social life:

> FREEMAN: . . . Observe but any morning what people
> do when they get together on the Exchange, in West-
> minister Hall, or the galleries of Whitehall.
> MANLY: I must confess there they seem to rehearse
> Bayes's grand dance. Here you will see a bishop bowing
> low to a gaudy atheist; a judge to a door-keeper; a
> great lord to a fishmonger, or a scrivener with a jack-
> chain about his neck; a lawyer to a sargeant-at-arms; a
> velvet physician to a threadbare chemist; and a supple
> gentleman usher to a surly beef-eater; and so tread

round in a preposterous huddle of ceremony to each
other, whilst they can hardly hold their solemn false
countenances.

FREEMAN: Well, they understand the world.

MANLY: Which I do not, I confess.   [I, i]

While the satirist's attack is upon hypocrisy, he touches
tangentially upon other vices. We are made to see that hypocrisy is the central core of a general cultural decay. Thus
his full complaint is that traditional in Roman satire—the
loss of the old ways when degree was observed and each
class respected itself and all other classes. Just as Juvenal
is moved to wrath again and again by the elevation in society
of a freed slave "whose razor scraped my youthful beard," so
Manly is disgusted by the sight of a great lord bowing to a
fishmonger. Loss of degree means loss of function. A bishop
who bows to an atheist does so not out of regard for the man,
but out of fear, or hope of gain, or as the consequence of his
own loss of religion. The falsity of social commerce is both
the cause and effect of the decay of social function. The par-
ticipants in the Bayes's dance are hollow men, and even the
dance itself is a pretense; the dancers can barely hold their
false countenances.

Act I, then, establishes Manly and Freeman in their key
roles and outlines the design that will be repeated throughout
the play with increasingly complex modification. The structure of *The Plain Dealer* does not follow a linear progression.
There is no real plot line that in its unraveling reveals the
theme. What "story" there is—the deception of an advocate
of truth by the only two people whom he had trusted and his
attempts to revenge himself upon the woman who wronged
him—merely provides excuse for the establishment of the
structural relationship upon which the play really hinges—
that of satirist, adversarius, and background. This design is
qualified by a satiric substructure, and the thesis is completed

in the final undoing of the satirist. However, in the first three acts the bare design is maintained but is progressively widened in scope until the field of satiric vision appears to be universal.

In Act II, besides setting up a satiric substructure that will be discussed later, Wycherley both expands the satiric background and "proves," in the action that he sets before us, the spoken satire of Act I. We become aware here of the great advantage of the dramatic mode over verse as a medium for realizing formal satire. The verse satirist is restricted in what he can display to the reader by the persona of his satiric spokesman. In the first place, he can present only as much as the satiric persona can see and comment upon, and, if he wants to preserve unity of structure, he cannot allow his spokesman to range too far. In the second place, the personality of his spokesman acts as a filter through which the background scenes must pass. For example, a scene of sexual corruption may seem to the reader to illustrate the perverse pleasure that the spokesman takes in describing sexuality, rather than to show the just rationality of his position as satirist. Consider the confusion to which this has led in the case of Swift. The satirist who chooses the dramatic mode, on the other hand, can not only present us with background at firsthand, so that we may observe for ourselves the justice of the satiric spokesman's position, but also present background in the descriptive scenes, anecdotes, character descriptions that appear in the conversations of characters other than the satiric spokesman. These are the means Wycherley employs in Act II to expand his satiric background. He allows free rein to three barb-tongued commentators upon high society: Olivia, Novel, and Plausible. In their repartee the satiric vision with which we had been presented in the Act I exchanges of Manly and Freeman is both widened and intensified. It is widened because Olivia and company focus their attention upon a new segment of society. We are introduced to the circles of the great, to the "Sir Richard Court-titles" and "Sir John Currents" of the world. It is intensified because we are taken into drawing and conference rooms to see hypocrisy at work. In Act I Manly and Freeman had discussed the most common, mildest form of hypocrisy, men's actions toward one another in public places. Now we see hypocrisy as the tool of the social climber and politician. To succeed in high society, we learn, a man must wear many masks, must indeed change his spots several times a day. Olivia describes the activities of one such man of mode:

> he endeavors only with the women to pass for a man of courage, with the bullies for a man of wit; with the wits for a man of business, and with the men of business for a favorite at court; and at court for city-security.
>
> [II, i]

However, satire in these scenes is double-edged. At the same time that Olivia, Novel, and Plausible are, in their discourse, enlarging the scope of the satiric background that had appeared in the Act I dialogue, they are proving the truth of it in their actions; while they speak, they are revealed to the audience to be hypocrites as great as the objects of their sharp wit. For example, Olivia, who opens Act II with a declaration to Eliza that she hates flatterers and is herself incapable of flattery, turns face upon the entrance of Novel and Plausible. In protesting the quiet simplicity of her life, Olivia denies knowing Novel and asks her maid to admit him on the pretext that he must be an acquaintance of Eliza. But when Novel enters and, preparing to begin his catty review of the company he has just left, asks the conventional "d'ye know whence I come now?", Olivia proves to be quite adept at flattering, "From some melancholy place, I warrant, sir, since they lost your good company." Novel and Plausible, thinking themselves rivals for Olivia's affections alternately

flatter and backbite one another. Olivia overtly pours the
sweet oil of flattery upon both, and roundly libels each in
asides. A further dimension is added to their hypocrisy by
the fact that each hates in the others the faults of which he
himself is most guilty. Olivia, for instance, joins Novel and
Plausible in criticizing absent friends, criticizes Novel and
Plausible behind their backs, yet complains of Novel, in an
aside, that he is the kind of coxcomb who "rather than not
rail, will rail at the dead." None of this company can be
other than false. Each of them uses flattery in some way to
enhance himself, either by gaining the admiration of others,
or worse, in the hope that others will prove in some way
useful. Only Manly escapes Olivia's flattery, for having already used him, she wants to be rid of him.

Act II works primarily upon the satiric background,
widening its scope and proving the spoken thesis in dramatic
action. But it also enlarges the subject of the satire itself; it
considers the various aspects of hypocrisy. For instance, in
Act I we are shown that on the personal level hypocrisy
makes genuine friendship between two men impossible,
while on the social level it renders fraudulent commerce
between the social classes. In Act II we are further shown
that hypocrisy forges masks behind which human beings
hide from one another and under cover of which they dupe
and manipulate one another. Olivia rebuffs all Eliza's attempts to drop pretense. She uses Novel and Plausible not
only in the cause of self-aggrandizement, but for gain. She
pretends affection for them, as she had for Manly, for money.
Freeman, the more blithely open opportunist, pursues the
Widow Blackacre for her jointure. Every human relationship, as well as every class relationship, is infected with the
distorting disease of hypocrisy.

In Act III the satirist and adversarius are once again in
the central position (they appear in Act II, but, for reasons
that will be discussed later, are not in the central position).

This act puts all three components of satire before the eyes of the audience, for the satirist and adversarius operate *within* the satiric background instead of projecting it from their discourse. The dramatic scene is indeed one of the scenes described in the spoken satire of Act I, which is now realized in action. There is no plot requirement which demands that Manly appear at Westminster Hall; nothing that he does there furthers the action, in the usual sense. However, the scene answers to perfection the demand of the satiric form for a crowded, moving background presenting one after another scrambling knave to provoke and to justify the satiric spokesman's fiery outbursts. The seat of justice, we find, is the scene of the greatest of all hypocrisies. Justice is a mere cover-up for self-seeking; the law a game of which only the lawyers can be winners.

A dominant figure at Westminster is the Widow Blackacre. A humour character thrown in partly for comic effect, the widow nevertheless embodies the spirit of the scene. Her life is an entanglement of the trappings of the law. She is weighed down with briefs, writs, and legal jargon, yet she has not the slightest conception of the meaning of justice. The law for the widow, as for the other denizens of Westminster, is a socially acceptable way of deceiving one's fellows for one's own gain. She spends much of her time training her lumpkin son, Jerry, "in the law"—that is, in the ways of turning every legal circumstance to profit. She has a maxim for every emergency. For example, if a lawyer proves unreliable, her advice is "let your adversary fee 'em, for he may chance to depend upon him, and so in being against thee, they'll be for thee." She neither understands nor values any good but material good. She will, for instance, deny her integrity on the spot, declaring herself an adulteress and her son a bastard, to protect her jointure and thereby her life in the courts. Yet even this prodigious lady of the law is no match for the double-dealing sharks of Westminster.

Despite all her maneuverings, her lawyer will betray her interest to solicit the favor of a lord.

> WID: Mr. Buttongown, Mr. Buttongown, whither so fast? What, won't you stay 'til we are heard?
> BUT: I cannot, Mrs. Blackacre, I must be at the council, my lord's cause stays there for me.
> WID: And mine suffers here.
> BUT: I cannot help it.
> WID: I'm undone.
> BUT: What's that to me?
> WID: Consider the five pound fee, if not my cause; that was something to you.
> BUT: Away! Away! pray be not so troublesome, mistress; I must be gone.
> WID: Nay, but consider a little; I am your old client, my lord but a new one . . .
> BUT: . . . will you be thus impertinent, mistress?   [III, i]

The inhabitants of Westminster cannot be appealed to but by promise of profit. They recognize neither contract nor justice nor old acquaintance in the face of an opportunity for gain.

Freeman flourishes in this atmosphere. It is here that he plans to ensnare the widow, declaring that he is sure that he is "the first man that ever began a love intrigue in Westminster Hall." It is altogether fitting that he should be so comfortably within his element in this atmosphere that he is able to conduct a love intrigue, especially since the object of his passion is the widow's money. While Freeman thrives in the country of opportunism, Manly is beside himself with rage. After he has incurred three law suits for boxing the ears of two lawyers and pulling the alderman's nose, he hits upon a method of exposing the hypocrisy of the law sharks and ridding himself of their noxious flattery at the same time. To each who approaches him he offers the opportunity of aiding the cause of justice without hope of gain. To the first he offers the case of a poor orphan who has lost her inheritance, a case that must be handled *in forma pauperis;* the lawyer, of course, recalls some pressing business that must have his immediate attention. An alderman who offers to buy Manly a dish of coffee finds himself presented with the prospect of standing security for a poor man, and he, in turn, is called away.

It is said that the reason Wycherley set Act III at Westminster is that he himself had been a student of the law. This external consideration is less important than the internal demands of form. We have observed the enlargement of the basic satiric pattern from Act I to Act II and have watched the opposing points of view operating in an ever-widening background. The scene at Westminster broadens the field of the satiric vision to the widest scope possible in drama. The mild flattery that glosses over the emptiness of social form in Act I, that masks snarling backbiting and personal manipulation in Act II, becomes in Act III the means to pervert justice. Here hypocrisy is a methodized approach to brutish self-seeking. We observe the poet uncovering the full dimensions of hypocrisy in an almost Platonic progression that traces the taint from falsity in personal relations, to distortion in social and class relations, to the corruption of an abstract principle, justice, upon which rules for the government of nations depend. The satire assumes universal scope and the final impression is of the whole world engaged in a frantic Bayes's dance of hypocrisy. This, then, is the widest development of the basic satiric structure as it appears in the play. Had Wycherley accomplished no more than to embody this design in drama, he would yet have answered the Restoration's demand for the reinstitution of classical form in satire. However, he goes further and builds into the structure of the play a satiric substructure that both extends the thesis of the satire by diminishing the character of the satiric spokesman himself and questions the very premise upon which satire rests.

The completion of the thesis, the destructive argument of the satire,[1] as well as the Elizabethan convention of the satyr-satirist demand that Manly be exposed as a practitioner of the vice against which he rails. His full disgrace occurs in the last two acts, where the focus is narrowed from the universal field of justice and trained upon the soul of a single human being. However, the deterioration of Manly's character is prepared for as early as the second act. As we have seen, Act I sets before the audience the three basic elements of formal satire in classic relation. It prepares the audience for formal satire; a Restoration audience would not have mistaken that intention. At the end of Act I Manly, whose part we have taken against Freeman, makes ready our introduction to Olivia. He tells us that she is as honest as she is beautiful, that she is possessed of every virtue, that she is the female counterpart of an honest man. The second act opening, then, is something of a shock. Instead of the womanly paragon we had been led to expect, we find in Olivia an imitation Manly, a parody-satirist. Her opening lines, "Ah! cousin, What a world 'tis we live in, I am so weary of it," affect a discontent that comes as an echo to Manly's protestations of world-hatred which we have just heard. More surprising still, a new satirist-adversarius relationship is established between Olivia and her cousin, Eliza, that imitates the Manly-Freeman relationship of Act I. Olivia rails against the world, its vanities and falsity, all the while proclaiming herself a plain-dealer. Eliza, in classic juxtaposition to Olivia, subtly baits her by drawing her into contradictions.

---

1. The classical design requires only that the scene be a total indictment of man, not that the spokesman be revealed a hypocrite. This latter is the contribution of the Renaissance satiric theory that we examined in Part I of this chapter.

ELIZA: But what d'ye think of visits—balls?

OLIVIA: O! I detest 'em!

ELIZA: Of plays?

OLIVIA: I abominate 'em, filthy, obscene, hideous things . . .

ELIZA: . . . what d'ye think of the court?

OLIVIA: How, the court! the court, cousin! . . . my aversion of all aversions!

ELIZA: How! the court where—

OLIVIA: Where sincerity is a quality as much out of fashion and as unprosperous as bashfulness: I could not laugh at a quibble, though it were a fat privy-councellor's; nor praise a lord's ill verses, though I were myself the subject; . . . nor sit to a vain young smile-maker, though he flattered me. In short, I could not glout upon a man when he comes into a room and laugh at him when he goes out: I cannot rail at the absent to flatter the standers-by. I—   [II,i]

In frankness, in tone, even in cadence, this speech of Olivia is a glaring imitation of Manly's "I cannot wish well . . ." speech of Act I. The whole exchange parodies the earlier Manly-Freeman exchanges. But, to our surprise as the verbal encounter between the two women progresses, we realize that an ironic reversal has occurred. The satirist, Olivia, who endlessly protests her virtue, is a hypocrite. The adversarius, Eliza, who makes no claim to be a champion of truth, is a plain-dealer. Step by step, Eliza forces Olivia into contradictions that expose her virtue as mere affectation. Her professed simplicity and scorn of outward show, for example, are laughed out of court when Eliza reminds her of the six dresses that she buys each month. Her mask of virtue and innocence slips when, Eliza leading her into discussion of *The Country Wife,* she proves herself expert at detecting double entendre. At the entrance of Novel and Plausible her exposure is completed. Olivia proves herself a hypocrite by her own terms, well able to "glout" upon a man when he comes into a room and laugh at him when he goes out, quite willing to rail at the absent to flatter standers-by. From Eliza's final commentary upon Olivia's affectation of plain-dealing —"railing is now so common that 'tis no more malice but the fashion"—we are led to suspect that attacking hypocrisy is itself hypocritical.

However, despite this reversal the *roles* of satirist and adversarius are maintained. The opening of Act II on the surface reproduces perfectly the Act I exchanges of Manly and Freeman. Olivia in her speech, manner, tone is the satirist; Eliza in her function of baiting, drawing comment, exposing, is the adversarius. Only the inner, moral positions of the contestants are reversed. The question we must ask is what function this reversal serves in the design of the play. Olivia's role serves three functions. Superficially, her spoken satire reinforces and even widens Manly's spoken satire of Act I. Her description of the court, for instance, takes its place beside the scenes and descriptions projected by Manly's discourse of Act I as part of the satiric background. A more important function, however, is Olivia's resemblance to Manly, which, undercut by her falsity, renders Manly's role of public defender of truth somewhat suspect. We never appreciate the pomposity and opportunism of Henry IV until we see them parodied in Falstaff. Similarly, Manly's public righteousness that seems so golden in Act I tarnishes when it is imitated by Olivia in Act II. Moreover, the revelation of Olivia, demonstrating as it does the characteristic private personality of cruelty, exploitation, and participation in the very vice against which she rails, in combination with the public affectation of virtue, prepares us for the full revelation of Manly's character that is to occur in the last two acts. In Olivia we are given a foreglimpse of Manly *whole.*

Most important, however, the parody substructure is a commentary upon satire itself. Manly loves Olivia because she resembles him: "I knew he loved his singular moroseness so well as to dote upon any copy of it." Before he is disillusioned, Manly thinks Olivia honest, upright, above reproach, because he thinks she is exactly like him and he thinks himself above censure. Our recognition of Manly's high self-esteem makes us wary of satirists. We realize that the satirist by raging at the vice of others, claims by implication to be himself above vice. He thereby leaves himself open to that pride which leads to the inevitable fall. The downfall of Manly is required for the full expression of the satiric thesis. But for the satirist to *appear* in the play and to be exposed as a hypocrite serves the further function of questioning the very meaning of satire itself. The play, then, is not only a well-executed formal satire but also a satirization of satire. Wycherley mocks himself: "You rail, and nobody hangs himself; and thou hast nothing of satire but in thy face." (V, ii). And he builds into the very structure of his play the tempering qualifications of his art: "for railing is satire, you know, and roaring and making a noise, humour" (V, ii).

The final deterioration of Manly is accomplished in Acts IV and V when the tri-elemental design of satirist-adversarius-background is abandoned and the full focus of satire is concentrated upon Manly alone. He becomes more obviously a Morality Everyman, the subject of a study in the corrosive effects of hypocrisy upon an individual soul. We will recall that his fall occurs as the private personality of the satyr overwhelms the public personality of the satirist in his nature. Since the nature of Manly's fall has been treated in an earlier chapter, there is no need for recounting it in detail here. Let us merely review the course of his decline. He begins as a firm opponent of hypocrisy. But we soon find that his strength is hollow, since it rests upon his never having been personally challenged. At the reversal of his personal fortune he begins his experiment in deceit ("how hard 'tis to be a hypocrite") to hide a weakness in his character. Before long he finds deceit less troublesome to his conscience. Having succeeded in hiding his shame from Freeman, he goes on to use hypocrisy to mask his manipulation of Fidelia, his pawn in the game of seducing Olivia. And manipulation becomes in due time shameless exploitation. When his threat to cut Fidelia's throat if she will not pimp for him proves ineffectual, Manly bribes her with the promise that if she will get Olivia for him, by any means, he will allow her to stay with him. He knows that Fidelia is loath to go again to Olivia's apartments (she fears rape by Vernish), but he ruthlessly exploits her affection for him and uses to his own advantage the very qualities for which he had ridiculed her, her softness and fear of violence. In the depth of his decline Manly has come full circle; he is at last the very creature he had at first accused Lord Plausible of being—a hypocrite "like a common whore or pickpocket, dangerous to those he embraces."

The structural reversal of Manly's coming full circle to the pole opposite his starting position is accompanied by a second ironic reversal. In Act II Wycherley had Olivia affect Manly's virtues but showed her to be morally false. As Manly's character declines, it grows more and more similar to Olivia's. As she had consciously imitated his virtues, he, in the last two acts, unconsciously imitates her vices. For example, in hiding his true feelings from Freeman (Act III, end) he imitates Olivia's attempts to hide her feelings from Eliza (Act II, repeated to exaggerated effect in Act IV). In the scene in Olivia's apartments when Manly, hidden in the dark, watches Olivia's pursuit of Fidelia, he becomes her mirror image. In the first place his lust is kindled by the scene, so that the similarity of his to Olivia's bestial depravity is forced upon the attention of the audience.

But also, his criticism of her lust is exactly like Olivia's criticisms of Novel in Act II—that is, he blames in another the very fault that he cannot recognize in himself. The parody substructure, then, makes its final commentary upon the basic satiric design. Olivia's surface resemblance to Manly is reversed to reveal Manly's actual resemblance to Olivia.

With the final decline of Manly's character the satiric thesis is complete. When Manly's virtue is proven hollow and he is shown to be one of the company of hypocrites, the satiric vision is fulfilled. All the world, every level of society, even the metaphysical realm of abstract concepts is tainted with falsity. The disease of hypocrisy is not more widespread than it is deeply rooted; man is essentially corrupt, essentially beastly. The satiric thesis has become, as it must, an indictment of human nature. Yet the thesis, however elaborate, cannot alone complete the requirements of the perfect satiric design. The poet, Dryden warns, is bound by his form to give some example of virtue. In this play the virtue opposing the thesis, the satiric antithesis, is realized in the character of Fidelia. Most critics consider Freeman and Eliza "the comic standard"[2] of *The Plain Dealer.* They are supposed, because they "champion the naughty world,"[3] to represent the poet's point of view. But if we are not to mistake Manly's excessive misanthropy for the poet's view, neither are we to negate the play's satire by accepting the viciousness against which Manly rails as the standard upon which we are to judge him and the other characters. To accept the "naughty world" (and naughty seems hardly the adjective that lust, deceit, and the perversion of justice should evoke), to mistake for the poet's viewpoint the satiric thesis itself, is to pervert the whole thematic structure of the play. Still the critics have argued well that if Manly is too excessive to be a hero, Fidelia is too unreal to be a heroine. When *The*

2. Cf. Lynch, *The Social Mode,* p. 171.
3. Ibid.

Plain Dealer is considered "Restoration comedy," Fidelia is completely inexplicable. How in the Restoration world could there exist a woman who disguises herself as a page to follow her beloved to war, or who woos another woman on his behalf? Fidelia is indeed unreal; she is vestigial. But her very unreality, the incongruity of her presence in the satiric landscape, fills the demand for a satiric antithesis. We will recall that the antithesis must be the virtue that opposes the vice attacked in the thesis, that it is weak and is nearly overwhelmed by the vice against which it stands, and, that it is always an argument in favor of old-fashioned goodness.

Fidelia stands in the play as a symbol rather than a character. Her name identifies her as a Morality play figure who has undergone association with the romance tradition. Essentially, she is Faithful to Manly's Everyman. She represents the quiet virtue that follows behind Manly's braggadocio courage, never boasting its goodness, wishing only to serve. In the tradition of Everyman, Manly ignores the virtue close at hand and chooses to pursue a reflection of himself, an embodiment of his baser nature. Fidelia, however, remains true to her name, and after she has come near to being violated and then to being murdered, Manly at last recognizes her and gives her his soul to guide. As the embodiment of the antithesis, Fidelia is weak, hardly noticeable amid the vice that surrounds and threatens constantly to overwhelm her (for example, Manly's rage, Vernish's sexual excess). She is also symbolic in that her disguise, materially more real than those of the others, is spiritually less real. Hers, the most overt mask, hides only modesty and womanly virtue.

Beyond her function as a Morality figure, however, Fidelia serves a yet more important symbolic function. Wycherley has made of her an expanded allusion to a lost golden age. Like the world of innocent nature or primitive

virtue to which Horace and Juvenal look in their satiric
antitheses is the green world of nature and romance that
Fidelia recalls. It is impossible to miss the resemblance of
Fidelia to Viola of *Twelfth Night*. Like Viola, she loves a
man who loves another woman and who does not recognize
that she herself is a woman. Like Viola, she serves this man
and, though it breaks her heart, woos for him the other
woman, whose name, significantly, is Olivia. Like Viola she
is wounded in a duel, her true sex is revealed, and she is
rewarded for her loyalty by the affection of the man she
loves. Shakespeare, we will recall, was prized by the Restoration as the poet of nature. Wycherley uses Fidelia to call
into comparison with the vicious present that the thesis
treats the green, romantic world of the past. *Twelfth Night,*
one of Shakespeare's most romantic and most pastoral
comedies, brings into the bleak satiric landscape of *The
Plain Dealer,* the faint image of the shepherd. Fidelia is too
literary, too abstractly romantic to function as a character
in the company of the knaves and goats of the thesis. Her
purpose is anachronistic; she trails visions of a world where
love and loyalty are the standard, where true love overcomes
all obstacles and heals all wounds. We are forced to compare
Wycherley's Olivia, a lust-ridden witch, to the gently love-
sick Olivia of Shakespeare's pastoral scheme, to view Manly's
attempted rape against Orsino's sighing, moaning Platonism.
We are made sharply aware that the satirist is one who has
come from the shepherd's innocent world to the cities of
the plain. But the allusion is deliberately literary because in
The Plain Dealer, as in most of the best satire, the vision of
a golden, innocent past seems unreclaimable.

Though Fidelia, the satiric virtue, proves able to survive
in the corrupt, realistic world dominated by vice, she is by
no means able to effect a glorious happy ending. It is true
that she gets her man, and by showing him that there is one
honest heart in the world, rights his unbalanced view to

some extent. But their union is not accompanied by the restoration of order and government of love that the comic form requires. Olivia is exposed, but neither she nor Vernish is punished or banished. Rather the Widow Blackacre assures the survival of injustice by arriving upon the scene in time to advise Olivia that she can sue. Novel and Plausible get back the jewels they had given Olivia, but there is no suggestion that they will cease to be hypocrites. And, most important, Freeman's opportunism is not in the least shaken by the example of Fidelia. The adversarius' view remains intact, for Freeman sees in Manly's conversion the discontent's compromise with good fortune.

> MANLY: But if I should tell you [Fidelia] . . . that your virtue (since greater than I thought any was in the world) had now reconciled me to't my friend here would say, 'tis your estate that has made me friends with the world.
> FREEMAN: I must confess I should; for I think most of our quarrels to the world are just such as we have to a handsome woman; only because we cannot enjoy her as we would do.
> MANLY: Nay, if thou art a plain dealer too, give me thy hand . . .   [V, iv]

This, the note upon which the play ends, should give us pause. It should first remind us that Freeman's view, the view of the majority, still exists, untouched by the virtue of Fidelia. It should also remind us that not Freeman's worldliness but Fidelia's romantic loyalty has given Manly, the satirist, a ray of hope. (We might notice the difference from Molière, where sophistication *does* triumph.) But it should also make us question the permanence of Manly's cure. He embraces Freeman here as he had embraced Olivia at the beginning, for being a superficial copy of himself, a seeming plain-dealer. In its ending the play answers the last requirement of the satiric form. It provides a vision of the corrupt world; it provides an opposing example of virtue, but it remains open-ended. The decision whether to heed the satirist's harsh demand for moral reformation is left to the audience.

According to Pope, Wycherley claimed that he had written *"The Plain Dealer* at twenty-five [1665] and *The Country Wife* at two and thirty [1673]."[4] If this statement is to be considered more than the quirk of predating that afflicts most writers, we must conclude that the 1665 version of *The Plain Dealer* was drastically revised before its presentation upon the stage (ca. 1674). Quite apart from the question of borrowings from *The Misanthrope* (written 1666) is the larger question of Wycherley's development as a writer of satire. Not only is *The Plain Dealer* a more finished, more artistically complex work than *The Country Wife,* but it also indicates that Wycherley by the time he wrote it was so familiar with the classical structure of satire that he visualized it as an ideal form, abstracted from any particular ancient model. One intention of *The Plain Dealer,* as we have seen, is to satirize satire itself. This object is realized structurally; Wycherley undercuts the satiric design by means of a parody substructure. He shows thereby an amazing mastery of the abstract satiric form. *The Country Wife* can be considered the apprenticeship leading to that mastery, for it is an imitation (in the Restoration sense) of a particular satire. It is the penultimate step in Wycherley's progress toward perfect satiric form, that point at which he abstracted the spirit and form of a single model, Juvenal's *Sixth Satire,* and revitalized it.

Employing the new method of imitation, Wycherley *becomes* Juvenal and, transversely, Augustan Rome *becomes* Restoration England. Many of the characters and scenes— references which hitherto have been thought to be peculiarly

4. J. Spence, *Anecdotes* (London, 1820), p. 161.

of the Restoration period—grow from germ-ideas and suggestions of Juvenal. But, because Wycherley's approach is to be "not his Interpreter, but He," the Juvenalian seeds bear Restoration fruit. Pinchwife, the classically Restoration "jealous Husband" is the shape Wycherley draws upon Juvenal's Ursidius, the old whoremaster who, despite his knowledge of the world, is driven at last to marry (line 38). Lady Fidget, who is so adept at acquitting herself when she is surprised by her husband in Horner's arms, finds her origins in Juvenal's women who can employ "the colors of Quintilian" in just such a situation. The character of the country wife herself and the pivotal argument of whether ignorance and rusticity are any insurance of chastity are Juvenal's.

> You tell me of the high repute of some maiden who lives on her paternal farm; well let her live at Gabii and Fidenal, as she lived in her own country and I will believe in your little paternal farm. But will anyone tell me that nothing ever took place on a mountainside or in a cave?[5]   [lines 55–59]

Juvenal's question is answered in Margery's letter to Horner. Country methods may differ in style from those employed in the city, but they are as efficient in achieving their universally desired effect.

> I'm sure if you and I were in the country at cards together . . . I could not help treading on your toe under the table . . . or rubbing knees with you, and staring in your face, 'til you saw me . . . But I must make haste, my husband comes.   [IV, iii]

Margery's tone is, of course, different from that of Juvenal's persona; that is partly because of the latitude afforded by the

5. All references to Juvenal's *Sixth Satire* are to *Juvenal and Persius*, Loeb Classical Library, trans. G. G. Ramsay (rev. ed. Cambridge, Mass., 1950).

dramatic mode, but primarily because, in line with the new methods of imitation, Wycherley has revitalized his master in the prescribed way, giving him the voice, and indeed the eye, of a contemporary.

As striking as the appearance of Margery in Juvenal is the appearance of Horner himself. In Rome, of course, Horner has a somewhat different disguise, but he is at heart the same Horner, and he employs his disguise in any age to the same purpose.

> [The cinaedi] do women consult about marriage and divorce, with their society do they relieve boredom, from them do they learn lascivious motions and whatever else the teacher knows. But beware! that teacher is not always what he seems; true he darkens his eyes and dresses like a woman, but adultery is his design. Mistrust him the more for his show of effeminacy: he is a valiant mattress-knight: there Triphallus drops the mask of Thaïs.   [lines 16–26]

It would have been impossible, even in so supposedly licentious an age as the Restoration, to present a man disguised as a homosexual upon the English stage. Wycherley therefore recasts Juvenal's idea as Horner's design of using feigned impotence as a device for outwitting husbands. We also find in this passage the psychology of Sir Jasper Fidget that wives ought to be supplied with sexually disabled male companions as a relief from boredom and a preventive against serious temptation.

In addition to characterization, Wycherley recasts many of Juvenal's scenes in Restoration terms, or rather sees in Restoration life the recurrence of the very situations that fell under the eyes of the satirist in Augustan Rome. For example, Margery's goggling over the "player men," which at first glance seems a standard Restoration device (contrasting the country bungler with the polished cit and showing

the rapidity with which she adapts herself to pleasures of
the town) is to be found in Juvenal.

> When soft Bathyllus dances the part of the gesticu-
> lating Leda, Tuccia cannot contain herself: your Apu-
> lian maiden heaves a sudden and longing cry of ecstasy
> as though she were in a man's arms; the rustic Thymele
> is all attention, it is then she learns her lesson.
>
> [lines 63–66]

One piece of evidence to support the notion that the Restoration audience, more familiar than we with ancient satire,
recognized *The Country Wife* as an imitation of Juvenal
is that Dryden in translating the Juvenalian passage seems
to have had Margery Pinchwife in mind.

> The Country Lady in the Box appears
> Softly she warbles over all she hears
> And sucks in passion both at eyes and ears.

Other lesser targets, which in Wycherley seem so uniquely
of the Restoration period, come from Juvenal. For instance,
the folly of locking up one's wife is one upon which Juvenal
touches, "I hear all this time the advice of my old friends—
Keep your women at home, and put them under lock and
key. Yes but who will watch the warders? Women are
crafty . . ." Even the practice among ladies of honor of keeping players also seems universal. Mistress Squeamish's keeping a "little tragedian" appears first in Juvenal, "Other
women pay great prices for the favours of a comedian; some
will not allow Chrysogonous to sing; Hispulla has a fancy
for tragedians" (lines 73–75).

At one point Wycherley adheres almost too closely to
his model. There is a striking similarity between the scene
in which Lady Fidget and her company of honorable ladies
gather to drink and talk bawdy and the scene in Juvenal's
satire where women perform the rites of the *Bona Dea.* If

we do not recognize its source, Wycherley's scene is at
first glance a trifle unusual in the play. First of all, it seems
a somewhat awkward intrusion on the action, for not only
does it fit slightly ill with the scenes that precede it (not in
itself unusual, for there are three lines of action in the play),
but even in its own sphere it jars. It strikes a more serious
tone, different from that of other scenes in which the women
appear and it is more than a little disgusting, for even the
joy of the women in drink is pervaded with a gross sexuality
—"Dear brimmer, let me enjoy him first." As they become
drunk, the women discard their masks and shamelessly
acknowledge their virtue to be a disguise.

> L.F.: Our reputation! Lord, why should you not think
> that we women make use of our reputation as you men
> of yours, only to deceive the world with less suspicion?
> Our virtue is like the statesman's religion, the quaker's
> word, the gamester's oath, and the great man's honour;
> but to cheat those that trust us.
> SQ.: And that demureness, coyness and modesty, that
> you see in our faces in the boxes at plays, is as much a
> sign of a kind woman, as a vizard-mask in the pit.
> DAIN.: For, I assure you, women are least masked when
> they have the velvet vizard on.
> L.F.: You would have found us modest women in our
> denials only.
> SQ.: Our bashfulness is only the reflection of the men's.
> [V, iv]

Wycherley appears to forget for the instant that his thesis
is not, as Juvenal's is, the bestiality of women, but is rather
the incongruity between the affectation of virtue and inner
beastliness. Satiric play arises not, as in other scenes in which
the women appear, between surface manner and subsurface
motive, for here the characters drop all disguise and revel
in their vice. The openness with which they acknowledge

their faults threatens for an instant the dramatic medium. It is in its open commentary on brazen vice that the scene too closely follows Juvenal. Wycherley's manner threatens to become the direct attack of the verse satirist. His tone takes something of the disgust that Juvenal's persona feels at the obscenity of the scene before him, for the Juvenalian passage is, indeed, obscene. The "dear brimmer" of Squeamish and Fidget is the Priapian goblet of Juvenal's "Maenads" conducting their orgiastic rite. Then, inflamed with wine,

> What foul longings burn within their breasts . . . how drenched their limbs in torrents of old wine . . . there is no pretense in the game; all is enacted to the life in a manner that would warm the cold blood of a Priam or a Nestor. And now impatient nature can wait no longer; woman shows herself as she is, and the cry comes from every corner of the den, "Let in the men."
> [lines 310 ff.]

Wycherley's women have not the actual release of the orgy; they meet to drink and *talk* bawdy. But, drenched in wine, they too reveal themselves. And, significantly, the climax of their rite is also to "let in the men," for each confesses her knowledge that there is a virile man present—Horner. If they cannot, like Juvenal's women, actually enjoy him at the moment, they substitute the vicarious pleasure of confessing that they have enjoyed him in the past. Although Wycherley does justify his borrowing to the satisfaction of the letter of the new law of imitation by translating Juvenal's scene into Restoration terms, he misses the spirit of the law by violating slightly the unity of his own design to copy rather than emulate his model.

This is however his one (after all quite minor) fall from grace. While he is not yet as perfect in extracting the satiric skeleton completely clean of flesh as he would become in writing *The Plain Dealer,* he nevertheless does imitate in

accordance with the new rules. His object in imitating is
to render the spirit of Juvenal in Restoration terms, and in
this he succeeds admirably. Though he does take the germ
ideas of certain characters and situations from his master,
this is the inevitable consequence of writing with a single
model in mind. He does not after all borrow effects in the
manner of the Elizabethans, for the object upon which he
trains his eye is the structural design of *The Sixth Satire.*
In this satire Juvenal does not follow the usual pattern of
setting satirist and adversarius against a fixed satiric background. Rather, the poet's persona is satirist; he aims his
argument directly at the audience. The adversarius is "you"
understood, and is directly addressed by the poet's persona,
"You tell me of the high repute . . . ," "Tell me, why is . . . ,"
"Look at those who . . . ," "Hear what Claudius had to en-
dure . . ." The poet-satirist surveys the corruption of the world
and addresses his commentary to "you." He then goes on to
build further commentary upon his imagination of what
"you" will reply. The satiric background, therefore, is actually the scene presented in his commentary. The design of
The Country Wife imitates this structure. The satirist does
not appear as a character in the play; the adversarius is the
audience, and the scenes presented before us are the satiric
background. The result is that there is in the play neither
a central character nor a central action. Horner is most often
employed as the mouthpiece for spoken satire, for commentary upon the scene. But he does not occupy a central position, as Manly does. He is not present in every scene. Rather,
the action speaks for itself and is occasionally interspersed
with scenes of commentary. Horner is not sufficiently detached from the scene to be the satirist's persona. As we have
seen, his position is that traditional to the parasite-satirist.
He is prominent but not central. He is distinguished from
the other characters by his cleverness but he is nonetheless
of their number. All the characters, including Horner, serve

as instruments of satire, examples used by the poet-satirist to illustrate his vision of human corruption.

As there is no central character, neither is there a central action. There are, rather, three separate actions; that which concerns Horner's disguising himself as a eunuch and his success in that enterprise, that which concerns the efforts of Pinchwife to keep his young and ignorant wife chaste, and that which concerns Harcourt's attempts to win Alithea from her misplaced loyalty to Sparkish. The actions are arbitrarily related in the relationship of characters in one action with characters in another. For example, the Harcourt-Alithea-Sparkish action is linked to the Pinchwife action because Alithea happens to be Pinchwife's sister, and to the Horner action because Harcourt happens to be Horner's friend. The lines of action are, therefore, loosely, if cleverly, linked, and none of the three predominates. Time on stage is divided almost equally among them. One's interest is directed upon one sphere of action and after the satiric point is made is shifted to another. The unity of the play, therefore, is not the unity of comedy, which depends upon a linear unraveling of theme through plot, but the unity of satire, which allows the eye to range from one to another scene of moral decay, each an aspect or dimension of the vice under consideration.

The play opens, as satire must, with a declaration of the thesis to be argued. The vice in question is lust, but not lust simply. Rather, it is lust that disguises itself, assuming one or another mask, not out of deference to morality, nor out of shame, but that it may under the protection of a disguise enjoy greater freedom to operate. The thesis is not declared directly, because there is no satiric persona in the play to speak it. It is, rather, presented graphically. As the play opens, Horner and Quack are discovered discussing Horner's plan. Horner inquires whether Quack has been diligent in spreading the rumor of his impotence. Quack assures Horner that he has, but questions the wisdom of the plan.

HORNER: Dear Mr. Doctor, let vain rogues be con-
tented only to be thought abler men than they are,
generally 'tis all the pleasure they have; but mine lies
another way.

QUACK: You take, methinks, a very preposterous way
to it, and as ridiculous as if we operators in physic should
put forth bills to disparage our medicaments, with
hopes to gain customers.

HORNER: Doctor, there are quacks in love as well as
physic, who get but the fewer and worse patients for
their boasting; a good name is seldom got by giving it
one's self . . . Come, come, Doctor, the wisest lawyer
never discovers the merits of his cause till the trial; the
wealthiest man conceals his riches, and the cunning
gamester his play. Shy husbands and keepers, like old
rooks, are not to be cheated but by a new unpractised
trick; false friendship will pass now no more than false
dice upon 'em.   [I, i]

In this dialogue Horner is not expressing, as Underwood and
others have suggested, the duality of art and nature; his
subject is lust and hypocrisy. The "natural" Horner is a satyr,
his only art the art of deception. He is a hypocrite, not a
natural man, and certainly not a hero. He discards the ruse
of false friendship not because it is dishonorable but because
it does not work. We should not dream of suggesting that
Lady Fidget is the heroine of Wycherley's play. We are quite
certain of the author's attitude toward such a lady of honor;
she is a target of satire. Why, then, should we mistake his
attitude toward Horner? Horner spreads the rumor that he
is sexually harmless, so that he may more freely indulge his
lust. Lady Fidget spreads the rumor that she is virtuous to
the same end. The only difference between them is that
Horner pretends a negative quality (to be harmless where
he is most harmful), while Lady Fidget pretends a positive

quality (to be in possession of the most grace where she is graceless). True, Horner's is the less usual disguise. It is used to attract our attention, by its very outrageousness, to the incongruity between what human beings pretend to be and what they are. In the opening scene Horner is presented as an emblem, a grotesque exaggeration of the vice we are to watch for in the play. He is, in graphic terms, the declaration of thesis.

The thesis declared, the argument of it begins. Because there are separate actions, of equal importance, that attract our attention by turn to the various aspects of the vice, the scenes maintain a degree of independence from one another. This enables the satirist to turn the vice under consideration around on all sides, to attack it from as many angles as possible. Scene after scene is presented in which some new face of the vice is presented or some aspect already presented is more deeply probed. The movement is circular and continues until all of what Dryden calls the "members" of the central vice have been presented and developed to their fullest extent.

The four faces of disguised lust that the design examines are presented by the end of the second act. First, Horner is introduced to present lust in the mask of impotence, which secures it full freedom. Then Sir Jasper enters with the "ladies of honor," who flaunt their masks of modesty and virtue. Horner, having assumed the role of malcontent-satirist, sounds the depths of their virtue and suspects it to be shallow. When the ladies have gone, he announces his suspicion to Quack, rejoicing in their disguise as well as in the efficacy of his own.

> your women of honour, as you call 'em, are only chary of their reputations, not their persons; and 'tis scandal they would avoid, not men. Now may I have by the reputation of an eunuch the privileges of one, and be

seen in a lady's chamber in a morning as early as her
husband.   [I, i]

The scene that presents vice disguised as virtue is followed
by a brief interlude of commentary upon the satiric background. Horner, in the company of the wits, observes and
comments upon the immorality of the world. Into this commentary a new aspect of disguised lust is introduced in the
person of Pinchwife. Pinchwife hides and indulges his gross
carnality under the socially respectable façade of marriage.

> HORNER: But prithee, was not the way you were in
> better? is not keeping better than marriage?
> PINCH: A pox on't! The jades would jilt me. I could
> never keep a whore to myself.
> HORNER: So, then you only married to keep a whore
> to yourself.   [I, i]

Pinchwife's jealousy arises from the desire to maintain intact the socially sanctioned contract, supposedly based upon
mutual regard, which provides him his mask for the indulgence of lust. He neither loves nor trusts his wife, and surely
he does not esteem her. He chose her not for any virtue he
admired in her but for her prime fault, ignorance, which he
hoped would protect his own façade. His sole interest,
throughout the play, is in forcing her to preserve his "honor"
as a husband, which honor is as false as Lady Fidget's virtue
or Horner's impotence. In reality, Pinchwife is not a husband
but the keeper of a whore, a piece of property that he is
anxious to preserve to his exclusive enjoyment. Like Horner
and Fidget, he desires freely to indulge his lust under cover
of a carefully sustained respectability.

The last aspect of the vice presented is lust disguised as
innocence. Perhaps lust is too strong a word to describe
Margery's emotion, as innocence is too imprecise to define
her ignorance. Her innocence at first is genuine. However,

once she has fallen in love with Horner, she develops guile, and she feigns innocence to disguise her passion from Pinchwife in the hope that she will thereby find the freedom to satisfy it.

In their first appearance the four aspects of the vice are almost purely comic—Horner's knavery, Fidget's affectation, Pinchwife's jealousy, Margery's rusticity are at first follies. However, at each successive appearance they assume more serious proportions, and by gradual stages the comic tone fades, to be replaced by the satiric. It is highly illuminating of Wycherley's method to trace the course of one aspect of the vice in its development. For example, let us consider lust disguised as virtue. Fidget and her company are wholly comic in their first appearance. They are objects of satire only in their folly of exaggeration—theirs is the "humour" of virtue which is threatened by Horner's wit. In Act II, a new dimension of their viciousness is revealed; their hidden lust, until now only suspected, is uncovered, and with it their whole perverted system of morality.

> L.F.: But, poor gentleman, could you be so generous so truly a man of honour, as for the sakes of us women of honour to cause yourself to be reported no man? No man! And to suffer yourself the greatest shame that could fall upon a man, that none might fall upon us women by your conversation? but, indeed, sir, as perfectly, perfectly that same man as before your going in to France, sir? As perfectly, perfectly, sir?
> HORN: As perfectly, perfectly, madam. Nay, I scorn you should take my word; I desire to be tried only, madam.   [II, i]

In the system of values that prevails in the world attacked by the satiric thesis, the greatest honor accrues from building the most complete disguise of one's real motives. Horner is a man of honor because by means of his deception he has ensured free sexual indulgence not only for himself, but for "the sakes of us women of honour." His generosity is in permitting for them the same license he permits himself. Moreover, within this moral system, the "greatest shame that could fall upon a man," is to be sexually incapacitated while perfection rests upon sexual prowess. Here, as in *Love in a Wood*, Wycherley makes his satiric point in the incongruity between the heroic diction of the speakers ("I desire to be tried only, madam") and the base matter of their speech. Their style captures perfectly the duplicity of their characters. While the incongruity between vehicle and tenor produces a largely comic effect, the perverted morality of the speakers—measured as it is against the ideal of the satiric antithesis—introduces a strong satiric undertone.

The next appearance of the women of honor is in the famous "china" scene of Act IV. So farcical is the scene, and so perfectly sustained its double entendre, that we are sometimes distracted from its satiric intent by our admiration of Wycherley's technique. If we consider the scene in relation to the others in this line of action, however, we realize that the women who at first affected grotesquely exaggerated virtue, and who at their second appearances could still discuss sexuality only in heroic periphrasis, here become ardent pursuers of Horner. We must not allow the comedy of the scene to blind us to the realization that it is but a hair's breadth short of presenting the sexual act on stage. Yet, as the predatory sexuality of the women more fully reveals itself, so the mask with which they disguise it becomes more pronounced. One minute after their hot pursuit of Horner they are gasping in horror to their gulled guardians,

> L.F.: O Lord, here's a man! Sir Jasper, my mask, my mask! I would not be seen here for the world.
> S.J.: What, not when I am with you?
> L.F.: No, no, my honour—let's be gone.

SQUEAM: Ah grandmother, let's be gone; make haste, make haste, I know not how he may censure us.

[IV, iii]

The last appearance of the women, in Act V, is the scene described above, which Wycherley models so closely upon Juvenal's rite of the *Bona Dea*. Here the comic tone vanishes completely, for the women, literally and figuratively, drop their masks and do not bother to affect virtue. The stylistic tension between diction and character no longer claims our attention. Instead, satire darkens and damns more directly. Wine has robbed the women of their disguises. They abandon elevated diction and manner. Their tone coarsens and becomes sluttish. As drink loosens their tongues, they damn their husbands and compare them to "old keepers." Their talk, that of prostitutes, indicates that they think of themselves in imagery of commerce ("Women of quality, like the richest stuffs, lie untumbled and unasked for"). And finally, in the passage quoted above, each of them acknowledges that she has enjoyed Horner.

The same progress from comic to satiric is described in the successive appearance of each of the three other aspects of the central vice. Pinchwife's jealousy is ridiculous when he is the butt of the wits' teasing. It becomes a more serious defect when we observe him abusing his wife. In its next appearance, when he threatens "write as I tell you or I will write whore with this pen-knife in your face," it has darkened into cruel sadism. Until, at last, it is distorted into frenzy that drives him to attempt the murder of Margery—a disaster that is averted only when his reputation as husband is rescued by the public assurance of Horner's eunuchry. Following exactly the same pattern, Margery's disguise, at first so charmingly funny, leads at last to her willingness to sacrifice Alithea's reputation in order that, saving her own, she may indulge her passion for Horner. And Horner's knavery, at first so devilishly clever that it escapes our censure, degenerates into mean knavery when at last he sacrifices Alithea's true honor to the preservation of his false disguise.

The satiric thesis is complete when we see that in this world of knaves and gulls the gulls are not a jot the more sympathetic company. Wycherley preserves the unity of his design by using the gulls to "transiently lash" (as Dryden puts it) vices related but subordinate to the main vice. Sir Jasper as a husband bears some resemblance to Pinchwife; he, too, values the reputation of husband alone. It is one part of the public image of which he is so careful and so proud. Sparkish is the male counterpart of Lady Fidget; as she is a would-be lady, he is a would-be man. Her disguise is false modesty, his is false wit. He values Alithea only as as an ornament to his reputation and an addition to his wealth. Sir Jasper and Sparkish, the gulls, are then hypocrites. Their hypocrisy differs from that of the other characters only in that it does not disguise strong, animal vice. But they are as contemptible for being hollow men, masking emptiness with a bright façade, as the other characters are for being goats.

The satiric thesis, then, is presented in successively reappearing scenes of vice and folly. With each turn of the spiral, new depths of the vice under consideration are disclosed. But we do not fully gauge the depravity of this world of inverted moral values until we contrast it with the standard presented by the satiric antithesis. The opposing virtue in this play is embodied in Alithea and Harcourt. The argument of the antithesis is stronger here than in most satires. Virtue is presented as a human possibility, not a quaint reminder of the past. Alithea and Harcourt are the twin virtues that oppose the double vice of the thesis. Alithea, as her name suggests, is the truth that opposes hypocrisy; Harcourt is the romantic love that stands against lust. For every aspect of vice presented, the opposing virtue is held up for comparison in

Alithea and Harcourt. For Margery's dishonesty clothed in ignorance is Alithea's sophisticated honesty. For Sparkish's foppery is Harcourt's manliness. For Pinchwife's jealousy is Harcourt's absolute faith. The scenes of vice are underscored by corresponding scenes of virtue. For example, Lady Fidget's and Horner's "perfectly, perfectly" exchange is immediately followed by a scene in which Harcourt tries to express in the disguise of double-faced diction his honorable passion for Alithea. Even though Harcourt's romantic love is the exact opposite of Horner's and Fidget's animal sexuality, Alithea will not allow even honorable love to go masked. She exposes Harcourt again and again to Sparkish. Again, the scene in which Margery disguises herself, at the risk of Alithea's reputation, to satisfy her passion for Horner is balanced by the scene in which Alithea tries to unmask Harcourt, who has come, disguised as a parson, to prevent her marriage to Sparkish. She insists upon exposing him even at the cost of injuring herself as well as Harcourt whom she has come to love. Horner, Fidget, or Margery will do harm to others by their lies in order to protect themselves. Alithea, on the contrary, sacrifices her own feeling, her love of Harcourt, to keep the contract she has made with Sparkish. Hers is the true honor which holds abstract principle above passion—the honor of the romantic heroine of pastoral that has dwindled in breadth, if not intensity, to fit the satiric design. It is against Alithea's true honor that we must measure the empty reputation of the gulls and the masked vice of the knaves.

Harcourt brings the ideal of romantic love into the design of the play. The scorn of marriage that is supposed to typify "Restoration comedy" has no place in this play. It is not marriage but false marriage that we must despise here, as we had despised it in *The Gentleman Dancing Master*. We are to scorn marriage as a commercial arrangement (Sparkish's view), marriage as a social accoutrement (the view of

Sir Jasper and Lady Fidget), and marriage as the outlet for
bestiality (the view of Pinchwife). These falsities must be
discarded in the face of the marriage that Harcourt offers—
marriage based upon romantic love. Harcourt assures Alithea that the love he offers her is "matrimonial love." He
describes his passion (III, ii) in the elevated diction of romance. He loves "with all his soul," prizing her above titles
or fortune. He offers himself as the man "who can only
match your faith and constancy in love," "who could no
more suspect your virtue, than his own constancy in his love
for you." When the test of Alithea's virtue comes, Harcourt
is willing to ignore reputation, and thereby proves that his
faith matches Alithea's virtue.

> AL: O—unfortunate woman! A combination against
> my honour! which most concerns me now, because you
> share in my disgrace, sir, and it is your censure, which
> I must now suffer, that troubles me, not theirs.
> HAR: Madam, then have no trouble, you shall now see
> 'tis possible for me to love too, without being jealous;
> I will not only believe your innocence myself, but make
> all the world believe it.   [V, iv]

Harcourt and Alithea, as their discourse here suggests, are
the faithful shepherd and shepherdess. Although the transition in the focus of Wycherley's vision from St. George to
the dragon has been effected, nevertheless in the satires, as
in his first pastoral, his standard of virtue is romantic. As we
have seen, even in *The Plain Dealer,* where the satiric vision
is perfectly achieved, the ideal, though it is envisaged as a
lost ideal, is romance. It is against the ideal standard of
romance that we must consider the satiric thesis—Pinchwife's socially sanctioned lust, Sparkish's vanity, the bestiality
of the ladies of honor, and Horner, their stud. As in all satire
vice is manifested in new-fangled manners—men pose as

eunuchs, women have drinking parties—while virtue lies in old-fashioned simplicity.

However, though virtue proves more attractive than vice, the satiric design must be preserved. Though the antithesis is stronger here than in Wycherley's last, most perfect satire, *The Country Wife* is, nevertheless, a well-wrought satire. Consequently, like *The Plain Dealer,* it is open-ended. Alithea and Harcourt will presumably live happily ever after in their virtue, but so will Horner, the Fidgets, the Pinchwifes live on as happily in their vice. Horner and the ladies come dangerously close to exposure, but by Quack's intervention their deception is maintained. The life of lust and hypocrisy is therefore assured both for Horner and the ladies. He has learned no more than never to trust his secret to a fool. Dorilant and Sparkish are so wrongly impressed by the example of the happy lovers that they vow never to marry. Sparkish is completely untouched by his experience: "Because I will not disparage my parts, I'll ne'er be [a husband]." His interest, as it has been from the beginning, is the façade he presents. Pinchwife learns only that the cover he had chosen to indulge his lust proves to be only an irksome burden. The example of Harcourt and Alithea is lost upon him. He has not learned what a true husband is, but only that his husband disguise is uncomfortable. He hates his wife more heartily than ever, but now he must keep her to serve the ends of reputation rather than lust. "I must be a husband against my will to a country wife, with a country murrain to me." *The Country Wife* presents the alternatives, ugly vice and beautiful virtue, but, in accordance with the demands of the satiric form, leaves the choice to the audience.

The evidence, then, points to *The Country Wife* as an earlier play than *The Plain Dealer.* It was composed with the structure of a particular Roman satire in mind, while *The Plain Dealer* was constructed upon an abstract model, an ideal of classical satiric structure. In addition, the proportion of romance to satire, though well within the boundaries of the classical form, marks *The Country Wife* as transitional from the early plays to Wycherley's best achievement. Both the satires, however, are important landmarks in the history of English satire. They represent the last application of Elizabethan theories of satire and the first appearance of neoclassical Augustan satire. They are pivotal works. To label them "Restoration comedy" is to lose not only the plays themselves but an important link in the chain of English literary history.

If this study has achieved its aim, it should prove that a writer of the Restoration period can yield riches if we approach him with our minds cleared of cant about the naughty age and clichés about "Restoration comedy." Wycherley is only chronologically of the Restoration period. From the beginning of his career he wrote in traditions that antedate and stretch far beyond the forty-year period to which we have confined him—traditions that are the very foundations of our literary heritage. The stones that went into his best achievement come from Anglo-Saxon, medieval, and Renaissance English, as well as Roman, ground. His mature plays span the gap between the two great ages of English satire and point to the highest achievement in this genre, the satire of the Augustan Age. The friendship between the old Wycherley and the young Pope, over which biographers have sentimentalized, may be considered a human relationship symbolic of the continuity of the English literary tradition.

Index

DATE DUE

APR 1 4 1972			
GAYLORD			PRINTED IN U.S.A.